BUBONIC PANIC

San Francisco's Chinatown
during the plague outbreak

BUBONIC
PANIC

WHEN PLAGUE INVADED AMERICA

GAIL JARROW

CALKINS CREEK
AN IMPRINT OF HIGHLIGHTS
Honesdale, Pennsylvania

For information about permission to reproduce selections from this book,
please contact permissions@highlights.com.

Calkins Creek
An Imprint of Highlights
815 Church Street
Honesdale, Pennsylvania 18431
Printed in China

ISBN: 978-1-62091-738-1

Library of Congress Control Number: 2015953543

First edition

10 9 8 7 6 5 4 3 2 1

Designed by Red Herring Design
Production by Sue Cole
Titles set in Knockout and Veneer
Text set in Caecilia LT

CONTENTS

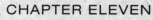
The flea

CHAPTER ONE
8   PHANTOM KILLER

CHAPTER TWO
12 PANDEMIC!

CHAPTER THREE
24 RETURN OF THE SCOURGE

CHAPTER FOUR
32 SECRETS UNCOVERED

CHAPTER FIVE
41 INJECTIONS OF HOPE

CHAPTER SIX
50 FLEAS AND FLAMES

CHAPTER SEVEN
62 DEATH IN CHINATOWN

CHAPTER EIGHT
76 THE MONKEY DIED

CHAPTER NINE
90 QUARANTINE OUTRAGE

CHAPTER TEN
100 NO END IN SIGHT

CHAPTER ELEVEN
108 CHANGES AT THE TOP

CHAPTER TWELVE
119 EARTHQUAKE!

CHAPTER THIRTEEN
128 BLUE'S BRIGADE

CHAPTER FOURTEEN
140 INTO THE WILD

CHAPTER FIFTEEN
152 DISEASE UNDEFEATED

167 FREQUENTLY ASKED QUESTIONS
172 GLOSSARY
174 TIMELINE
176 FOR MORE INFORMATION
180 AUTHOR'S NOTE
182 SOURCE NOTES
188 BIBLIOGRAPHY
193 INDEX
197 PICTURE CREDITS

DEDICATION

For Heather, who piqued my interest in plague

ACKNOWLEDGMENTS

I appreciate the assistance of everyone who helped me investigate, understand, explain, and organize the story of plague's arrival in the United States. Thanks to Dr. Kenneth L. Gage, Division of Vector-Borne Diseases, Centers for Disease Control and Prevention, for answering my questions about plague, suggesting resources, and making helpful comments; Dr. Matthew Frye, New York State Integrated Pest Management Program, Cornell University, for sending me journal articles about fleas and plague; Ethan Degner, Department of Entomology, Cornell University, for sharing his flea expertise with me; and the reference staff at Cornell University Library for locating hard-to-find resources.

Writing a manuscript is only part of the long, complicated process of producing a book. Thanks to the talented Calkins Creek crew for their creativity, inspired suggestions, hard work, reliability, and attention to the smallest detail. I'm particularly grateful to my editor, Carolyn P. Yoder, for the many big and little things she does to make sure a book is the best it can be. No author could ask for more.

—GJ

PHANTOM KILLER

> "We see death coming into our midst like black smoke . . . a rootless phantom which has no mercy."
>
> —Jeuan Gethin, fourteenth-century poet

The killer was a master of stealth. It moved undetected, sneaking from victim to victim and always catching its targets by surprise.

Their end usually came after three or four horrific days of suffering. For a few—the ones spared that agony—life drained away in hours.

In the beginning, the killer traveled slowly. But before long, it stormed through cities, towns, and the countryside on a rampage, leaving behind more death than anyone had ever seen. Terrified, many people fled, abandoning their homes and neighbors and even their families.

The killer's signature was unmistakable, though it went by different names: The Plague. The Pestilence. The Great Mortality. The Black Death.

If you were a victim, you felt sick within two to six days.

First came the high fever, throbbing headache, achiness, weakness, chills, and sometimes nausea and diarrhea. These symptoms weren't unusual at a time when countless maladies and diseases afflicted humans. But when you saw the grotesque swellings, you knew your body had been attacked.

The painful lumps under your skin seemed to pop out overnight. You'd find one or more, usually in your armpits, on your neck, or in your groin. Called *buboes*, from the Greek word for "groin," the swellings were often the size of a chicken egg. They could grow as large as an orange.

At least three of every four victims developed buboes. You were lucky if you were one of them. Even though the bubonic form of plague was fatal for 40 to 60 percent of victims, it was your *best* chance of surviving.

Your odds were far lower if you had septicemic plague. The early symptoms were similar to bubonic, but instead of buboes, you saw dark purple blotches on your skin from bleeding under the surface. In some places, blood flow was disrupted, particularly on your nose, fingers, or toes. Gangrene might set in and turn your skin black. Your organs failed. Septicemic victims rarely recovered.

The killer had a third way to slaughter its victims. With pneumonic plague, you fell ill one to four days after the attack. You had a high fever, chest pain, and a cough. You struggled to breathe. You spit up blood. A red froth surrounded your lips. Within a couple of days— or even hours—you'd be gone. Death might come so fast that you'd go to bed healthy and never wake up.

Like a phantom haunting the land, the killer took the lives of the lowliest beasts to the greatest human leaders. It was powerful enough to defeat mighty armies, change history, and determine the fates of countries and their people. Nothing stopped it. The wisest physicians were no match. Potions and remedies failed to cure. Prayers and incantations couldn't slow the murderous advance.

And while millions died, the killer's secrets remained hidden.

SIGNS OF PLAGUE

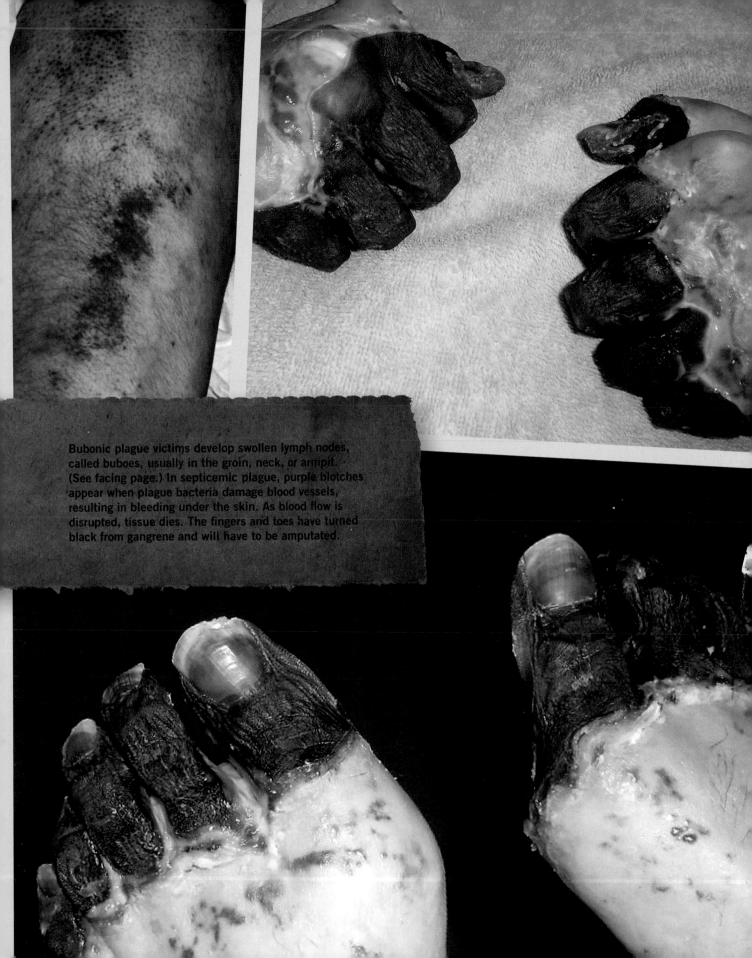

Bubonic plague victims develop swollen lymph nodes, called buboes, usually in the groin, neck, or armpit. (See facing page.) In septicemic plague, purple blotches appear when plague bacteria damage blood vessels, resulting in bleeding under the skin. As blood flow is disrupted, tissue dies. The fingers and toes have turned black from gangrene and will have to be amputated.

CHAPTER TWO

PANDEMIC!

> "This is the end of the world."
>
> —*Agnolo di Tura, 1348*

The sick left to die. Corpses piled high. Cities decimated. Fifteen hundred years ago, a devastating disease cut a swath of death across the world. Survivors wrote of the dark days when "the whole human race came near to being annihilated."

Epidemics had overpowered mankind before, though their causes would never be known for certain. But this time, the scourge left incriminating clues on the victims' bodies, and the witnesses to the carnage would never forget them.

A WORLD DOOMED

In the year 542, the historian Procopius wrote of the horror in Constantinople (now called Istanbul, in Turkey). The bustling city of a half million residents was the capital of the Byzantine Empire, the eastern half of the Roman Empire.

In gruesome detail, Procopius described a new, mystifying disease that started with sudden fever. Soon a "bubonic swelling" and black blisters appeared. He saw people vomiting blood and dying a few hours later. Some victims, he wrote, fell into "a deep coma, with others a violent delirium" that caused them to run out of their houses, "crying out at the top of their voices."

Tombstone from graveyard in Eyam, England, a village devastated by plague in 1665

Physicians had never seen an illness like it. They didn't know how to treat or prevent it.

Most people believed there was little *anyone* could do about the "pestilence." God sent it as punishment for their wicked, sinful behavior.

All work stopped. Fields lay untended and animals unfed. Markets closed. Those who endured the disease died of starvation.

Bodies lay unburied and rotting for days in Constantinople's streets, because no friends or family were left alive to place them in tombs. In a nearby city, gravediggers ran out of vacant earth in which to bury the dead. They stacked corpses in the towers of the city's fortifications, creating "an evil stench." In some towns, survivors tossed bodies onto boats for dumping at sea.

The epidemic lasted about four months in Constantinople. At its height, 10,000 people died each day. By the time it ended, 20 to 40 percent of the city's population was dead.

Procopius heard that the pestilence had come from Egypt the year before. Eventually, he wrote: "It embraced the entire world, and blighted the lives of all men . . . respecting neither sex nor age."

SLOW TO DISAPPEAR

Many historians and biologists believe that the plague pandemic started in central Asia. Once the disease reached the eastern Mediterranean Sea, ships carried it throughout the region. Plague spread to the Middle East, the Persian Empire (Iran today), and Western Europe, probably traveling with traders and armies over both land and sea routes.

Even after the original wave of death ended in the sixth century, smaller outbreaks continued in Europe and the Middle East, maybe for as long as two hundred years. Some reports claim that plague reached India and China, though historians don't have enough medical and historical records to confirm it.

Today, this widespread outbreak is known as the Justinian Pandemic, after Emperor Justinian I, who ruled the Byzantine Empire in the sixth century. Before the pandemic ended, plague likely killed tens of millions of people out of a world population of about 200 million. The body count remains a guess.

Then, after terrorizing humans for generations, the killer mysteriously went into hiding for nearly six hundred years.

Justinian I, as he appears in a mosaic created around 547 A.D. inside a church in Ravenna, Italy. The First Pandemic is named after him.

Plague killed so many people so fast that the dead were buried in mass graves.

WAVES OF HORROR

In 1345, a Mongol army laid siege to a fortified Crimean town on the shores of the Black Sea. Caffa (today called Feodosia) was a major trading post run by merchants from Genoa, Italy. The Mongols, whose trade routes stretched from central Asia to southern Russia, wanted control of the port.

Sometime during 1346, bubonic plague broke out in the besiegers' camps, killing most of the soldiers. The Mongols abandoned their siege.

Caffa wasn't out of danger, though. Inside the town walls, people began to fall ill with the same ghastly disease afflicting their enemy. Italian merchants in Caffa later claimed that the Mongol army infected the town by catapulting corpses over the walls.

With plague raging in Caffa, some of the Italians fled the epidemic on ships. But there was no escape.

Their ships traveled across the Black Sea, stopping in Constantinople on their way to the Mediterranean Sea and Italy. By early summer 1347, many of the sailors were dead and plague had broken out in Constantinople. As the ships continued on to European ports, including Sicily, Venice, and Genoa, they brought disease with them.

According to one fourteenth-century writer, "The sailors, as if accompanied by evil spirits, as soon as they approach the land were death to those with whom they mingled."

The relentless killer spread from port cities into the interior of one country after another until it cursed much of the world. From 1346 to 1353, the "Great Mortality"—as Europeans called the epidemic at the time—raced through Europe, parts of western Asia, the Middle East, and North Africa.

Hundreds of years later, these first seven years of the Second Pandemic became known as the "Black Death." The name might refer to the black marks on the victims' skin or to the dark dread that people felt during this horrifying period of history.

Plague survivor St. Roch, depicted in a religious painting with a bubo on his thigh. He was said to have miraculously healed many plague victims in fourteenth-century Italy.

TOO MANY CORPSES

An Irish monk, Friar John Clyn, told of plague's arrival in his country in 1348: "Many died of boils and abscesses, and pustules on their shins or under their armpits; others died frantic with the pain in their head, and others spitting blood." In 1349, Friar John succumbed to plague himself.

A Welsh poet, Jeuan Gethin, described the bubo:

"It is seething, terrible . . . a painful angry knob. . . . Great is its seething, like a burning cinder. . . . It is an ugly eruption that comes with unseemly haste. It is a grievous ornament that breaks out in a rash. The early ornaments of black death." Gethin and his seven sons all died of plague.

The disease killed with shocking speed. Parents woke children each morning with fear that the buboes had suddenly appeared on their small bodies during the night.

Agnolo di Tura, a resident of Siena, Italy, buried five of his children in a single grave after plague overtook his city from May to October 1348. "Very wide trenches were made," he wrote, "and in these they placed the bodies, throwing them in and covering them with but a little earth. After that they put in the same trench many other bodies . . . and so they laid them layer on layer until the trench was full."

Both Christians and Muslims believed that the plague was sent by God, the same view shared by their ancestors during the Justinian Pandemic. Others were convinced that the Great Mortality was unleashed by a special alignment of Mars, Jupiter, and Saturn. Or maybe it was a comet or an earthquake that brought on the pestilence.

Physicians and scientists had their own explanation: Plague, like all diseases, was caused by miasmas—foul-smelling, poisonous air from rotting plants and animals. Miasmas entered the body through skin or by breathing. When the sick exhaled, they contaminated the space around them.

Doctors tried their usual remedies to rid a patient of these impurities and restore the body's balance. Bleeding with leeches. Purging the bowels with enemas. Using ointments of blood and feces. Placing toads on the buboes to suck the plague's poison. And if those didn't do the trick, cutting open the buboes so that the poison drained from the body.

None of these disgusting treatments worked.

People were desperate to escape from the miasmas. The best ways? Drive away the dangerous vapors with smoke by puffing on

According to some accounts, more than 1,000 victims of the 1665 London plague epidemic were buried in this churchyard pit.

a pipe or setting fires. Block out the foul air with sweet-smelling herbs and flowers or strong-smelling camphor and spices. Some doctors wore elaborate headgear packed with these miasma-blocking plant materials.

But many people were convinced that wasn't enough. They believed if you touched the food of an afflicted person or the items he handled, you would catch the disease. If he looked at you, plague would strike you down. The pestilence might get you even if you thought about it.

The only way to save yourself, they decided, was to avoid both the polluted air and the sick. Lock yourself in your house, and remain there. Better yet, if you had the money and means, get away as far and as fast as you could.

Scottish writer John of Fordun described how his fellow countrymen reacted when the pestilence arrived in 1350: "Men shrank from it so much that, through fear of contagion, sons, fleeing . . . , durst not go and see their parents in the throes of death."

TOP: The protective clothing worn by medieval plague doctors. BOTTOM: A woodcut shows people fleeing London during a plague outbreak in the early 1600s. Skeletons hold arrows, a symbol of plague. The hourglasses indicate that time is running out.

STAY AWAY!

When people couldn't cure or outrun plague, they tried to contain it. Authorities shuttered the houses of the sick, leaving the victims inside to die. They burned contaminated clothing and mattresses of the dead to destroy the harmful miasmas that rose from them.

If plague struck a small village, neighboring communities isolated it and stopped anyone from going in or out. In many towns, authorities examined visitors arriving by land for plague symptoms before letting them enter.

Port cities required ships coming from an infected area to anchor far from shore and remain there for forty days. This isolation was called a *quarantine*, based on the Latin word for "forty." The time period had its roots in religious tradition. It may also have been based on the length of time it took, according to physicians, for an infected person to show signs of a contagious disease and either recover or die.

Despite attempts to stop it, plague kept up its brutal attack. It wiped out families. It emptied villages. Thousands of houses sat abandoned, their owners dead. Cities and towns fell into chaos.

The disease killed indiscriminately. The rich and poor. Clergy. Doctors. Government officials. Even royalty—including a Spanish king and queen, a French queen, and an English princess.

People felt helpless, and soon they looked for someone to blame. Christians and Muslims blamed each other. Both groups blamed Jews. In Switzerland, France, Germany, and Italy, thousands of Jews were massacred, accused of poisoning wells with plague to murder Christians. The accusers didn't seem to notice or care that Jews were dying of plague, too.

Plague in 1665.

Workers collecting bodies during the London plague smoked pipes to ward off dangerous miasmas.

THE DEATH COUNT

Where and when did the Second Pandemic start before plague arrived in Caffa? The truth is buried in the past. Reliable records from many parts of the world are limited, and their writers did not describe disease symptoms the same way they're recognized today.

Plague may have reemerged in central Asia during the first half of the fourteenth century. Then it traveled with traders and armies to the Black Sea, where the Mongol army besieged Caffa.

To find out how many people died, historians examined church and government census reports before and after plague struck a community. They counted bodies in burial pits and cemeteries. Records are unreliable and incomplete for some areas and missing for others, so it's impossible to be exact.

According to the best estimates, during the Black Death of 1347 to 1353, at least 20–25 million people died of plague in Europe. That was one-fourth to one-third of the population. A few historians put the number closer to half. In the Middle East, at least one-third of the population died.

In some cities, the death toll was even higher. Florence and Siena, Italy, each lost about 60 percent of their residents. In Jarrow, England, plague killed 80 percent.

During the next four centuries, periodic plague outbreaks snuffed out the life of millions more in Europe and the Middle East. The disease might have been reintroduced to those regions several times by land travelers and ships. Some historians think that near the end of the Second Pandemic, plague may have spread through China and India, too, though that view is controversial.

The last Western European outbreak occurred in the French port of Marseille from 1720 to 1722. Tens of thousands died, nearly half the city's population. After that, plague seemed to disappear.

But the killer wasn't through with humans. It would show its face again, slaughtering millions. And next time, it would invade cities and countries that hadn't even existed during the Black Death.

Human skulls and bones in a European plague pit from the Second Pandemic

CHAPTER THREE

RETURN OF THE SCOURGE

> "The Chinese are not the only people in the world who loathe cleanliness and sanitation in any shape or form."
>
> —The Lancet, 1894

In mid-January 1894, Mary Niles, an American missionary doctor working in Canton (now known as Guangzhou), China, was called to the home of a Chinese general. His daughter-in-law had awakened with a high fever and an extremely painful boil in her groin. Could Dr. Niles help?

Niles examined the Chinese woman. The symptoms looked like a case of typhus. Nothing unusual for Canton. The young woman eventually recovered, and Niles didn't think much more about it.

During the following weeks, however, the doctor saw seven more patients with the same symptoms. Then some news made her reconsider her original diagnosis. Canton officials were collecting thousands of dead rats throughout the city. One of Niles's young patients fell ill with fever and swellings after visiting a house where thirteen dead rats had been found in a single morning.

Niles had heard an old Chinese warning that a great rat die-off was an omen of a human plague epidemic. She grasped the alarming

connection to her patients: "Rats in infected houses [of sick people] have died." Her patients hadn't had typhus. The swellings in their groins were *buboes*. It was plague!

THE THIRD PANDEMIC

Niles's diagnosis in Canton might have been the first by a Western doctor. But the earliest signs of a new plague pandemic occurred forty years before and hundreds of miles away, in Yunnan Province of southwestern China. Historians now point to the 1850s as the beginning of the Third Pandemic.

Why did plague reappear after staying concealed for so long? Like the many other mysteries surrounding the disease, no one knows exactly how, when, or where plague struck humans again.

The Canton riverfront in 1900 is jammed with shantyboats, the homes of thousands of people.

From Yunnan, it spread east through southern China, moving with travelers along land and river trade routes.

In January 1894, shortly before Niles saw her first case, plague showed up in the busy river port of Canton. By March, it had become an epidemic.

Victims developed a high fever and excruciating buboes in the armpits, neck, thigh, or groin. Many fell into a coma, dying a day or two later. According to some accounts, as many as 40,000 to 80,000, out of nearly 2 million people, died during the Canton outbreak. An official count was never made, however, and these numbers might be too high.

By early May, plague was on the move again, invading the British colony of Hong Kong, 75 miles (120 kilometers) away.

POISON

Hong Kong's British authorities were worried. The colony's economy depended on international trade. Out of fear of plague, some countries might ban products coming from Hong Kong. Shipping companies could refuse to use the busy port.

In 1894, Western physicians, including those in Hong Kong, knew little more about plague than fourteenth-century doctors. When word of the outbreak reached London, an article in the

Workers at Hong Kong's busy wharf pull a cart loaded with cargo.

respected British medical journal *The Lancet* said: "That there is some poisonous substance connected with the causation of this disease it is scarcely possible to deny." But the experts had no idea what the poison was or how to stop it from sickening people.

A crowded Hong Kong
street market, around 1900

The medical community believed that infectious diseases flourished in certain surroundings. Overcrowded homes and neighborhoods. Poor sanitation. Foul drinking water. Inadequate ventilation. Bad nutrition, especially the low-protein diet common in Asia. These conditions helped to spread this "highly contagious" plague poison, the same way they spread cholera, typhus, and typhoid fever.

The reports from Hong Kong seemed to confirm that. Most plague victims were poor Chinese laborers who lived in congested neighborhoods. According to one observer, "The houses are so filthy that they are unfit for human habitation."

British authorities saw only one way to stop the contagion: clean up and sanitize. The Hong Kong sanitary board began an intense anti-plague campaign. British soldiers gathered corpses left in the street. Knowing that the Chinese might not report illnesses to the authorities, inspectors checked every building in Chinese neighborhoods for sick and dead plague victims. They isolated the sick, away from friends and family, in crowded plague hospitals or on a floating ship in the harbor.

Each plague victim's house was cleaned with harsh chemicals. Floors and walls were scrubbed. Health experts believed that plague could be transmitted from one person to another by clothing, bedding, wool, and hair. So they sterilized a victim's furniture and belongings with steam or drenched them with disinfectant chemicals. If the sanitary board decided that a building or its contents were too dirty, the only option was to burn them.

Hong Kong authorities blockaded neighborhoods where infected people had been found. No one was allowed to enter or leave.

In Hong Kong, British soldiers clean out the homes of plague victims in 1894, burning furniture and other contents considered too dirty to sanitize.

ANGRY REACTION

Many of these anti-plague measures were the same ones used five hundred years earlier during the Black Death. Hong Kong's Chinese residents bitterly resented them. They didn't accept the British ideas about disease spreading among people.

A Chinese fishing boat in Hong Kong, 1896

The Chinese were furious when they heard that their dead were being cut open and examined by British doctors. To them, autopsies were barbaric. And why was it necessary to bury victims in mass graves covered with more than 3 feet (about 1 meter) of cement?

They didn't understand the reason for separating the sick from their families. What was happening to their relatives forced onto the plague ship? Rumors flew that European doctors were killing pregnant Chinese women and children.

Tens of thousands of Chinese fled the colony to China to escape the disease, the stringent regulations, and Western doctors. Others hid their ill friends and relatives so that they wouldn't be taken away to a plague hospital. Angry mobs threw rocks at sanitation teams.

By the end of 1894, the official hospital death toll in Hong Kong was about 2,700, mainly Chinese. Because plague victims often died without a diagnosis and many Chinese cases were never counted, the epidemic's fatalities were certainly higher. Still, accounts of 100,000 deaths out of Hong Kong's population of 246,000 are exaggerations.

Physicians didn't think Westerners in China had to worry about catching plague. As one prominent doctor told a newspaper, "It is a disease peculiar to the Orient, and seldom, if ever, attacks Europeans."

This statement proved to be incorrect. Some Europeans did get sick and die in Hong Kong, mostly British soldiers and healthcare workers. But far more Chinese residents were struck down, and they had little chance of recovering. The plague killed practically every Chinese person it infected and about two-thirds of the non-Chinese.

GERMS, NOT MIASMAS

Bubonic plague's sudden comeback shocked and terrified the world. Everyone had heard the awful stories of the Black Death. Was it about to happen again?

This time, plague might spread even faster and farther than in the 1300s. Modern steamships traveled the oceans to every corner of the globe at speeds surpassing anything fourteenth-century sailors could imagine. The world's population had nearly quadrupled, providing the killer with a billion more potential victims than during the Black Death.

But there was hope.

Louis Pasteur (1822–1895), in a famous 1885 painting by Albert Edelfelt.

Although doctors knew little about plague, the study of diseases had come a long way since the Second Pandemic. A new idea, called germ theory, had taken hold. Research by Louis Pasteur of France, Robert Koch of Germany, and others proved that microscopic organisms—not miasmas—made people sick. Better microscopes and new staining techniques enabled scientists to see these tiny microbes.

During the fifteen years before plague reached Hong Kong, these scientists had identified the microorganisms that caused tuberculosis, diphtheria, and typhoid fever. Using this knowledge, they developed treatments for diphtheria and typhoid and were working on preventative vaccines.

Because human plague had been hidden for so long, doctors and scientists hadn't had a chance to study it before. Now they could. They hoped the knowledge would help them fight the deadly disease before the world faced another Black Death.

CHAPTER FOUR

SECRETS UNCOVERED

> "I go on cutting and examining buboes."
> —Alexandre Yersin, 1894

In June 1894, just a month after the Hong Kong epidemic began, two researchers arrived in the colony, determined to solve plague's mysteries.

The men came from different countries and spoke different languages. But they shared the belief that through the science of bacteriology, they could discover plague's cause. Once they did, they would be able to prevent and cure a disease that had haunted mankind for millennia.

Shibasaburo Kitasato was born in Japan in 1853. As an outstanding medical student, he won the opportunity to study bacteriology in Germany under Robert Koch.

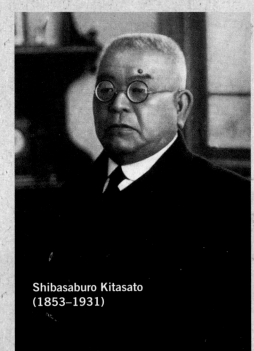

Shibasaburo Kitasato
(1853–1931)

During Kitasato's six years in Berlin, he helped develop ways to treat tetanus and diphtheria.

In 1892, Kitasato returned to Japan where he continued to search for disease cures. When plague broke out in Hong Kong, the concerned Japanese government sent Kitasato to study it.

He arrived in Hong Kong on June 12, 1894, supported by two top-notch researchers and three experienced assistants. The British doctor in charge of Hong Kong's main plague hospital, James Lowson, gave the Japanese team a room for their laboratory. They set up their equipment and got to work.

THE FRENCHMAN

Alexandre Yersin arrived three days later. He was born in 1863 in Switzerland and grew up there. His mother was French, and Yersin adopted French citizenship in his midtwenties.

Alexandre Yersin (1863–1943)

Although Yersin studied medicine, he never wanted to be a doctor with a private practice full of patients. In his opinion, "To ask for money for treating the sick is a bit like telling them, 'Your money or your life.'"

Instead, he took a job in Paris as a pathologist, preferring to spend his time in a laboratory. In 1886, a careless error changed the direction of his life.

While performing an autopsy on a person who had been bitten by a rabid dog, Yersin cut his hand and became infected with rabies. At one time, this would have been a death sentence. But the year before, Louis Pasteur and Émile Roux developed an effective anti-rabies treatment for humans.

Yersin hurried to Pasteur's Paris laboratory for help. Roux vaccinated him, saving his life.

The experience inspired the twenty-three-year-old Yersin. After his recovery, he left his pathology job to study bacteriology at the School of Medicine in Paris and with Robert Koch in Berlin. Later, Yersin worked with Roux at the Pasteur Institute in Paris, where they made advances in the treatment of diphtheria.

Alexandre Yersin wasn't the typical medical researcher, however. He wanted to travel and explore French Indochina (today the countries of Vietnam, Cambodia, and Laos). In 1890, he left Europe and took the position of physician on steamships in Southeast Asia.

When plague broke out in Hong Kong in 1894, Yersin knew he had to go there. He felt confident that he had the training and skill to tackle the frightening disease, just as he had diphtheria. "The first thing I shall have to do in the study of plague," he wrote in his journal, "is to look for its microbe." Hong Kong was the place to do it.

With help from his friends at the Pasteur Institute, Yersin convinced his government to send him to Hong Kong as part of the French colonial health service. In June 1894, he packed his bags and left Indochina on a cargo freighter.

Émile Roux (1853–1933)

THE RACE

Yersin landed in Hong Kong on Friday, June 15. He saw right away that he didn't have Shibasaburo Kitasato's connections. James Lowson refused to let Yersin near the corpses of hospital patients.

How could he do his research if he didn't have access to a victim's body? For Yersin, it was the essential first step: "More than anything, I would like to perform an autopsy."

He suspected he'd find the plague microbes in the victim's buboes, blood, and perhaps some organs. To identify these bacteria, Yersin would have to take samples and examine them under a microscope. He was aware that the Chinese were offended by autopsies. The only corpses he'd have a chance to cut open were those that the British made available, likely without permission from the deceased's family.

Yersin found himself in a race, one the Japanese apparently were determined to win. Lowson was doing all he could to support Kitasato, whom he considered a more influential scientist than Yersin. That included obstructing Yersin's research.

Without access to the main plague hospital's facilities, Yersin worked from a straw hut nearby. His laboratory consisted of a microscope and glass slides, an autoclave to sterilize equipment, scalpels for cutting, and cages of guinea pigs and mice.

Yersin soon learned that he might have lost the race before he even started. The day before he arrived in Hong Kong, Kitasato had found microscopic organisms in plague corpses. He injected these microbes into test animals, which died within days. When Kitasato checked their bodies, he saw the same microorganisms.

Proudly, the Japanese team declared that these were plague bacteria. About a week later, on June 23, 1894, *The Lancet* officially announced Kitasato's exciting discovery to the world.

It came with a steep price. Three of Kitasato's fellow Japanese researchers fell ill with plague, and one of them died.

Japanese researchers inject plague bacteria into rats. This photograph was taken in Japan about twenty years after Kitasato's work in Hong Kong.

TOO EARLY TO GIVE UP

Yersin was skeptical about Kitasato's claim. After visiting the Japanese lab, he concluded that Kitasato was on the wrong track. In his report to the Pasteur Institute, he wrote: "I am surprised to see that they are not even examining the bubo; rather, they are minutely investigating the heart, the lungs, the liver, the spleen, etc." Yersin felt sure that if the microbes were to be found, they would be in the buboes.

Kitasato's announcement added to Yersin's frustration. The Frenchman had already wasted five days trying to get access to a plague corpse. He was tired of dealing with Lowson and British red tape. On Wednesday, June 20, Yersin took action.

He walked over to the plague mortuary, an underground area outside the hospital where bodies were kept in cool temperatures before being buried. Two British sailors stood guard. They recognized the man who greeted them with friendly words when he passed by each day.

Yersin slipped them some money. Would they let him go inside? The sailors didn't hesitate. They unlocked the door and stepped aside.

Working quickly in the shadows, Yersin opened one of the caskets. He scanned the corpse for the telltale bubo. Pulling out his sharp scalpel, he cut away the swelling.

Yersin hurried back to his shack laboratory with the sample. Heart racing with anticipation, he prepared a slide with the bubo tissue and peered at it through the microscope lens.

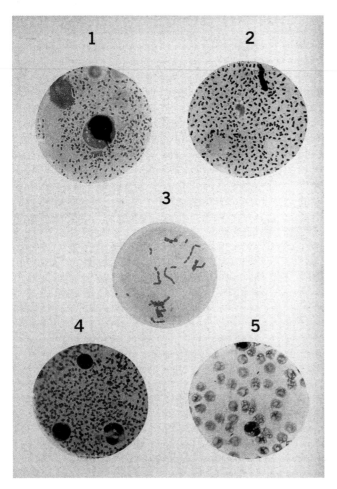

Images from Yersin's 1894 scientific paper show his microscope view of small oval plague bacteria in various tissue samples: (1) from a human bubo; (2) from a dead rat; (3) from a broth culture; (4) from a mouse; (5) from the blood of a man dying of plague with only two tiny bacteria visible among the round blood cells.

As the view came into focus, he felt the thrill of the moment. "The specimen is full of microbes, all looking alike, with rounded ends," he scribbled in his notebook. "This is without question the microbe of plague."

Yersin cultured the oval bacteria, then injected them into his guinea pigs and mice. The next day he wrote: "My animals inoculated yesterday are dead and show the typical plague buboes." When Yersin looked at samples of the animals' buboes and organs under his microscope, he saw the same oval microbes.

They were *not* the same bacterium Kitasato described. "The microbe isolated first by the Japanese," Yersin reported to the Pasteur Institute, "did not resemble mine in any way."

Yersin poses in front of the straw hut he used as his Hong Kong laboratory in 1894.

Yersin named the plague microbe *Bacterium pestis*, and the Pasteur Institute in Paris announced his discovery on July 30, 1894.

The public announcement irked Lowson. In August, he sent a letter to Kitasato, who by then had made his triumphant return to Japan. "I salute you and hope that you will be able to prepare a new shell filled with Pest Bacilli," wrote Lowson. "If you can at the same time kill a man called Yersin, for God's sake do so. He has led us a dance in a way but . . . we have got the better of him."

Lowson illustrated his note with a sketch of Yersin, making the Frenchman look like the devil.

The Yersin-Kitasato story didn't end there. Both men were recognized for finding the plague bacterium, though Kitasato received credit for beating Yersin by six days. Many British and American medical books acknowledged Kitasato as the true discoverer of the microbe, while the French gave the nod to Yersin.

But as Yersin realized in June 1894, the descriptions by the two bacteriologists were different in significant ways. Other scientists eventually found flaws in Kitasato's research. The bacterium he described does not cause plague. It causes pneumonia. Kitasato mistakenly incriminated the wrong microbe in his sample tissue from plague corpses.

Yersin's detailed description in June 1894 *had been* accurate. More than seventy years later, the microbe was finally renamed *Yersinia pestis* in his honor.

Several oval-shaped *Yersinia pestis*, highly magnified and stained to appear green

RATS AND MICROBES

Finding the plague bacterium wasn't enough for Yersin. He still had a hunch to investigate.

While walking around Hong Kong in June and July 1894, he noticed dead rats everywhere, even inside the plague hospital. Like Mary Niles, Yersin had heard the superstition about rat die-offs. What if it were true and plague killed these rats, too?

To find out, he collected rat corpses and took samples of their lymph nodes and blood. He examined the fluid under his microscope.

Amazing! There they were. The very same microbes he had seen in the bubo of the human plague victim.

Next, Yersin injected mice with these plague bacteria and placed the animals in a cage with healthy mice. The inoculated ones died. Within a few days, the rest died. When Yersin examined the dead animals' tissues, he found plague bacteria in all of them.

His hunch was right. Plague killed the rats, and it killed the healthy mice, too. Yersin had made an important breakthrough. "Plague is therefore a contagious and transmissible disease," he concluded. "It is probable that rats are the major vector in its propagation."

How did rats pass the disease to each other and to humans? That remained a puzzle.

FIGHTING THE GERMS

The discovery of the plague microbe during the summer of 1894 was hailed worldwide as a triumph by science and modern medicine.

The top U.S. health official, Surgeon General of the Marine-Hospital Service Walter Wyman, said of the news: "All through the centuries . . . [plague] has been enveloped in darkness, and there has been the same groping after facts, the same unsuccessful search for the true cause, the same struggle in ignorance against its ravages. . . . [It is now] robbed of its terror by science."

Doctors assumed that the bacteria spread from a victim's breath, blood, feces, and bubo pus. Rats spread it, too—to each other and to humans—by contaminating water, buildings, and soil. Going barefoot, as many Chinese did, allowed germs on the contaminated ground to enter the body through tiny foot cuts. To the medical community, this explained why fewer Europeans than Asians developed plague.

Health officials saw no reason to change their approach to plague outbreaks. Destroy the germs. Isolate the sick. Quarantine those exposed.

Several more years would pass before plague fighters learned there was a better way.

Meanwhile, plague kept moving. Hong Kong was a busy port where British steamships collected and delivered passengers and cargo. The disease wouldn't be confined there for long. Before anyone could stop it, plague found its way across the seas.

A Chinese sailboat and a British steamship in the Hong Kong harbor in 1902

CHAPTER FIVE

INJECTIONS OF HOPE

> "People . . . in Bombay are dying like flies from the plague."
>
> —Times of India, 1897

Dockworkers spotted the masses of dead rats first. Then people in the neighborhood close to the docks suddenly fell ill, dying within days.

By August 1896, plague had struck Bombay (today called Mumbai), India.

Even after doctors confirmed that plague was to blame, local officials swore it wasn't true. The 850,000 residents of Bombay knew better. "Every one who could escape to a place of refuge," said one person, "began to desert the city."

Train stations filled with panicky Indians loaded down with their belongings. Half the population fled. By early 1897, the streets were nearly deserted. Each day, death haunted those who stayed behind.

Men carry a deceased plague victim through Bombay in this illustration from *Harper's Weekly*, June 3, 1899. The long-lasting Indian epidemic caught the attention of the world's press.

RED CIRCLES

Plague's arrival didn't surprise Western medical experts who nervously watched it spread in China. Like Hong Kong, India was part of the British Empire, and ships regularly sailed between Hong Kong and Bombay on India's west coast. The British eventually convinced the doubting local Indian officials that something must be done. Otherwise, the disease would storm through Bombay the way it had in Hong Kong.

Indian and British medical and government authorities joined together to fight the epidemic with the same methods the British employed in Hong Kong. Officials forced the sick into plague hospitals. All of a victim's contacts were quarantined for ten days in a special health camp.

Soldiers painted red circles on houses and shops where victims lived or worked. They disinfected floors, walls, and sewers of these buildings with millions of gallons of carbolic acid. Afflicted neighborhoods were blocked off.

In 1897 Karachi, India (now part of Pakistan), a house is demolished after officials decide it is impossible to disinfect. Circles on the wall near the man on the right represent plague victims from that building.

The British gave up trying to control the city's extraordinary number of rodents. They decided it was easier and more effective to kill the germs.

In the hospitals, plague victims lay suffering in beds lined up along the walls. One visitor was overwhelmed: "All round one is met by cries, groans and delirious ravings."

So many plague victims needed hospital care that new patients had to wait outside until someone died and freed up a bed. They usually didn't have to wait long. "Sometimes we think a patient is recovering and we leave him for five minutes," said a nurse. "On our return we find him dead."

Indians noticed that fewer Europeans caught plague. They suspected that the Westerners were poisoning them. Some Indians believed that if you ended up in the hospital, your liver would be cut out and given to Queen Victoria, Great Britain's ruler. These fears drove even more people to run away from Bombay. Others rioted to protest the forced hospitalizations and disinfection campaign.

Those fleeing Bombay carried plague with them. To limit the spread within India, authorities inspected train passengers for signs of the disease. In certain cities, travelers weren't allowed to enter until they bathed and their clothes were disinfected by boiling.

A plague hospital in Bombay, 1896–97

Desperate people tried to find ways around the inspections. When authorities ordered one woman to be examined for plague, her husband refused to allow it. A fight broke out, during which the frantic man murdered the inspecting doctor and, unintentionally, his wife.

British soldiers and hospital staff disinfect a patient during the 1897 plague outbreak in Karachi.

The attempts to control plague failed. Within weeks, the disease reached several more Indian cities. Ships arriving from plague areas infected other ports, including Karachi (now part of Pakistan).

By the end of 1897, nearly 60,000 Indians had died. During the next dozen years, plague would kill 6 million of the country's 300 million people, most of them poor. In many Indian cities and rural areas, more than 8 of every 10 people died.

THE UKRAINIAN

While doctors and officials in India struggled to save lives, plague researchers jumped at another chance to find a cure.

Waldemar Haffkine arrived in Bombay just as the epidemic exploded. Born in 1860, he trained as a biologist in his native country of Ukraine, then part of the Russian Empire. As a university student,

Haffkine protested the restrictions imposed by the Russian czar on Jews like himself, and he was arrested several times. When he refused to renounce his religion and join the Russian Orthodox Church, Haffkine was banned from holding a university research position. His career as a biologist had reached a dead end.

Then, in 1889, he heard from a respected Ukrainian biologist with whom he had once studied. The man was conducting research at the Pasteur Institute, and he wrote to ask Haffkine to join him. Grateful for the opportunity, Haffkine headed to Paris.

Three years later, in 1892, Waldemar Haffkine made a name for himself by developing the first cholera vaccine. He had found a way to combat a disease that killed millions around the world. During a cholera epidemic in India, the British government invited Haffkine to inoculate tens of thousands of Indians.

He had been in India nearly three years when bubonic plague broke out in Bombay. In October 1896, Haffkine hurried to the port city, hoping to use his knowledge of vaccines to help.

**Waldemar Haffkine
(1860–1930)**

Haffkine (seated center) inoculates people of Calcutta, India, with his cholera vaccine in 1894.

NO TIME TO LOSE

Haffkine set up a makeshift laboratory in a room at a Bombay medical college. Working with an assistant and three helpers, he grew plague cultures and then destroyed the bacteria with heat. By injecting a solution of dead bacteria under the skin, Haffkine hoped to stimulate the body's immune system to defend against the microbe. If the vaccine was effective, the body would be prepared for an attack by dangerous live plague bacteria, too.

After three months of frantic effort, the vaccine was ready for testing. Haffkine injected his first subjects. Then he followed up with an injection of living plague bacteria.

His subjects stayed healthy. He had succeeded!

This test wasn't enough, though. Haffkine's subjects were rabbits. He proved that the vaccine would prevent a plague infection. But was it safe to give humans?

Testing the vaccine on a person was risky. Haffkine had to guess at the dose. And if the vaccine failed, or if any live bacteria survived the heating process, the person would come down with plague. The odds of death were high. He couldn't let anyone take that gamble.

There was only one solution. On January 10, 1897, Haffkine asked his assistant to inject him with the trial vaccine.

Six days passed. Haffkine kept track of his body's reaction. "My temperature went up . . . and generally a mild manifestation of the recognised symptoms of the plague," he noted. "Simply I felt somewhat out of sorts." He never developed a full-blown case of plague. Haffkine was satisfied that his vaccine was safe.

The next week he tried it on others. Plague had sickened 15 men at a Bombay prison, and 8 recently died. The disease was spreading. Prisoners were offered Haffkine's vaccine, and about 150 men accepted it.

Afterward, some of them had a fever and sore arm near the injection site, and 2 men came down with plague. They both survived. The only 3 who died after being inoculated already had swollen lymph glands when Haffkine injected them with the vaccine.

About 170 prisoners refused the inoculation. Of the 12 in that group who fell ill with plague, 6 died.

Haffkine was pleased with the results. "The benefits are twofold," he said later. "Inoculation prevents the disease, or, if the disease does attack a patient, renders it less virulent."

ONE NEW WEAPON . . .

Word of Haffkine's vaccine traveled around the world. For the first time, humans had protection from the scourge of plague.

As more people received the vaccine, Haffkine's confidence in it grew. Among those who were inoculated, many fewer developed plague after exposure to the disease. Of those who became sick, fewer died.

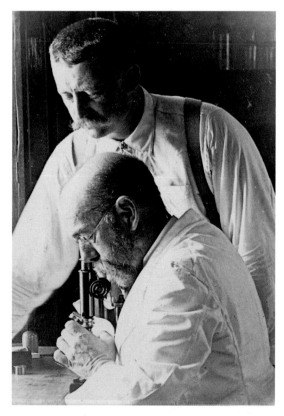

German bacteriologists Robert Koch (1843–1910), seated, and Richard Pfeiffer (1858–1945) traveled to Bombay in 1897 to study the plague epidemic.

But the deaths in the prison test showed that the vaccine was too dangerous to give to a person who was already infected. It could be used to *prevent* plague, but it could not *cure* it.

The vaccine helped protect doctors and nurses who cared for plague patients. Even if they later caught the disease, they usually had a mild case. One injection could last at least several weeks and perhaps up to several months. People who received multiple inoculations had even more immunity.

Despite the successes, some Indians refused to get the vaccine. False rumors circulated that it was made from cattle and pigs, offending India's Hindus and Muslims, who have strict religious beliefs about these animals. Many were suspicious because Europeans produced it.

Then, during the inoculation of hundreds of Indian villagers in 1902, an assistant dropped his forceps. He failed to properly sterilize them before he opened a bottle of the Haffkine vaccine, and it became contaminated. Nineteen villagers who were inoculated from that bottle died of tetanus. The incident frightened the Indian public and convinced people that the vaccine could kill.

Yet many Indians feared plague more than the vaccine. Within three years, at least 2 million people across the country received it.

. . . AND ANOTHER

Alexandre Yersin hadn't rested after discovering the plague bacterium. He returned to the Pasteur Institute and began the search for a plague cure based on the techniques used to make diphtheria antitoxin.

A laboratory at the Pasteur Institute in Paris, around 1910

Yersin and his fellow scientists developed a process in which plague bacteria were injected into horses. In most cases, the large animals didn't get sick, but their bodies produced substances to counteract the bacteria. These substances showed up in the horses' blood. To use them, Yersin separated out the clear yellowish blood serum and injected it into the patient's abdomen, back, or flank. Once in the human body, the substances helped fight off plague bacteria.

In March 1897, as plague raged in India and Haffkine was testing his vaccine, Yersin took the anti-plague serum to Bombay. It worked as a cure, though not as well as he hoped. The plague victim had to receive the injected serum within the first two or three days of illness. Otherwise, the serum had no effect. Many doctors questioned whether it could cure plague no matter when it was given.

The Yersin serum was used to prevent plague, too, especially in health workers and others exposed to the disease. The serum protected them only for two or three weeks, however. Many who received the injection developed a high fever and painful joints.

Despite the shortcomings of Haffkine's vaccine and Yersin's serum, they were the only hope the world had in its war against the lethal microbe.

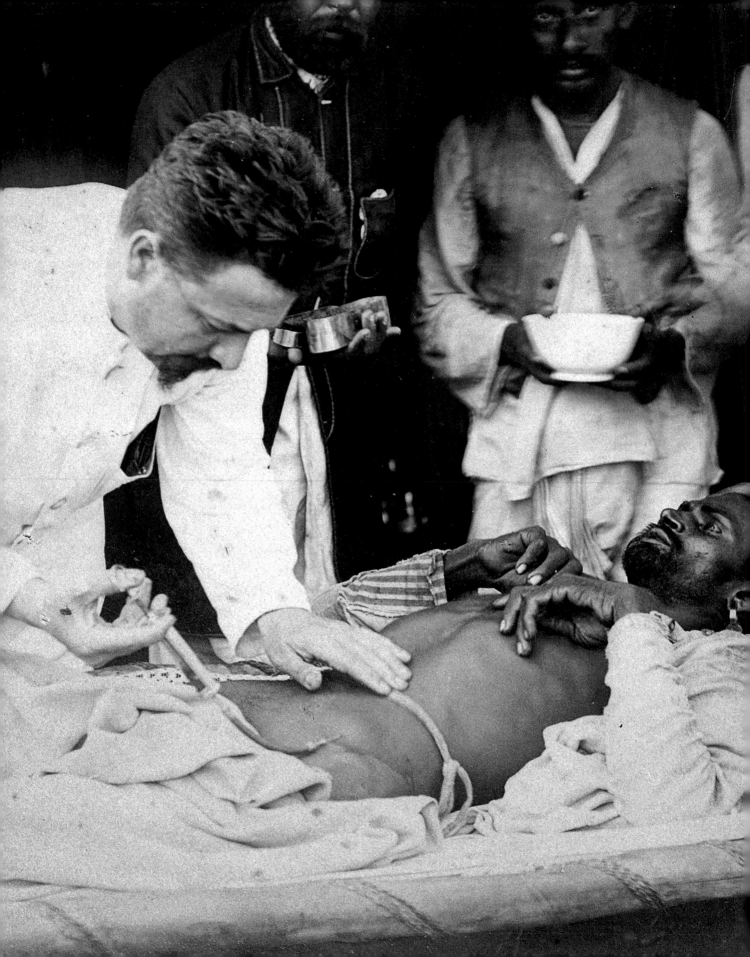

CHAPTER SIX

FLEAS AND FLAMES

"Modern quarantine . . . has proven, and will continue to prove, a powerful shield against this Asiatic invasion."

—Walter Wyman, 1900

After Yersin returned to Indochina, another bacteriologist arrived in India to treat local people with the anti-plague serum. Paul-Louis Simond, born in France in 1858, studied at the Pasteur Institute and served as a physician in the French Colonial Health Corps.

Simond was a careful observer, and what he saw and heard in Bombay made him question the way plague spread. He talked to people who witnessed an outbreak in their village or neighborhood. From them, he learned that victims often caught the disease even though they'd had no contact with another victim.

He knew about a Bombay factory where, one morning, workers found dead rats strewn across the floor. Twenty workers were told to get rid of them. Three days later, half of those men had plague. None of the other workers at the factory caught the disease.

Paul-Louis Simond (1858–1947) injects Yersin serum into a plague patient in India.

Then there was the Bombay man who found a dead rat in the stable near his horse one morning. Picking up the rat by its tail, the man tossed it outside. In three days, he was sick with plague.

WHAT ABOUT THE RATS?

By 1898, Simond began to doubt the accepted theory that plague spread among people through food, water, soil, and air. Like Yersin, he suspected rats were the key. That hypothesis raised many new questions.

Was it possible to catch plague just by coming close to a plague-infected rat?

Why didn't people get sick if they touched a rat that had been dead for more than a day?

Did rats carry plague from place to place? If so, how did they infect people?

Simond stumbled on an important clue when he noticed fleabites on the lower legs of several plague victims. Inside some of the bite wounds, he discovered plague bacteria. He knew that rat fleas occasionally bit humans. Was this how people caught plague from rats?

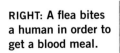

RIGHT: A flea bites a human in order to get a blood meal.

TOP: The flea takes in its host's blood.

Simond thought he had the answer. "We have to assume that there must be an intermediary between a dead rat and a human," he decided. "This intermediary might be a flea."

To test his idea, Simond became a rat-watcher.

In spring of 1898, he set up a laboratory that was even more primitive than Yersin's in Hong Kong. Under a tent, Simond carried out his investigations using a microscope and several cages of rats and mice.

He observed that healthy rats regularly groomed themselves and had few fleas. But when a rat became sick, it stopped this behavior and became infested with the insects. After a sick rat died, its fleas needed a new source of fresh blood. Where did they go to find their food?

Simond guessed that the fleas jumped off a dead rat's cooling body onto a warm, active rat. When no living rats were close, which happened during a die-off, the fleas chose another warm mammal passing by. Sometimes that was a human.

Did this explain why rat die-offs foretold a human plague outbreak? And why people became ill even though they'd had no contact with another human plague victim?

Xenopsylla cheopis, **known as the Oriental rat flea**

To find out, Simond became a flea-hunter. On the streets, he found a rat that had recently died from plague. Using forceps, he picked up the still-warm rat and placed it into a paper bag. The long handles of the forceps maximized the distance between the corpse and Simond's body.

He dropped the bag into warm soapy water and cut it open underwater. This prevented the fleas in the rat's fur from leaping onto Simond. He pulled a few drowned fleas from the fur and examined them with his microscope.

It was an astonishing sight! The fleas' digestive systems were teeming with plague bacteria.

When Simond examined the fleas on healthy rats, he found none of the microbes.

ZEROING IN ON FLEAS

For the next part of his experiment, Simond tested whether fleas carried these bacteria from rat to rat. He put a plague-infected, flea-infested rat in a tall glass jar, its top covered with fine mesh. Air came into the jar, but fleas could not escape.

A day later, while the rat was dying, Simond lowered into the jar a cage containing a healthy rat. Earlier, he determined that the rat's fleas, *Xenopsylla cheopis*, were able to jump at least 4 inches (10 centimeters). So he kept the cage at this distance while preventing the healthy rat from having direct contact with the sick one below.

Twenty-four hours after the sick rat died, Simond removed its corpse from the jar. He left the healthy rat inside the hanging cage.

After five days, the rat in the cage was dying of plague. When Simond did an autopsy on it, he discovered buboes and "abundant plague bacilli in the organs and blood."

Simond wanted to be sure that the healthy rat had been infected by plague bacteria from the fleas, not bacteria in the air. He repeated the experiment with one change. This time he removed all fleas from a sick, plague-infected rat before putting it in the bottom of the jar.

A healthy rat in the hanging cage did not get plague. And when Simond placed infected fleas back into the jar, the healthy rat developed the disease.

He'd been right. His experiments showed that fleas transmitted plague bacteria between rats. Fleabites on human plague patients were filled with the same microbes. This proved that the insects carried the bacteria to humans, too.

It was an important discovery in the fight against plague. Simond wrote in his journal: "I felt an inexpressible emotion at the thought that I had just uncovered a secret that had tortured humankind since the appearance of plague on the earth."

MORE PROOF

Simond wasn't the only one to solve this mystery, although he didn't know it yet. The year before, in 1897, a Japanese scientist made the same remarkable connection between plague and fleas.

Masanori Ogata had been an instructor of Kitasato's, the bacteriologist who raced Yersin to find the plague microbe. While working in Formosa (today called Taiwan), Ogata examined the fleas on a plague-infected rat. Inside each flea, he saw plague bacteria mixed with the insect's previous blood meal.

Rattus rattus (also known as the house, black, or roof rat) was one of the rat species that spread plague in India.

To test whether the bacteria could infect another animal, Ogata ground up the fleas and mixed them with a liquid. He injected the mixture into mice. The mice developed plague.

"One should pay attention to insects like fleas," Ogata later wrote in a scientific paper, "for, as the rat becomes cold after death, they leave their host and may transmit the plague virus directly to man."

The bacteria, Ogata noted, were identical to those Yersin described. Kitasato's bacterium was *not* the one that caused plague.

Even though Simond and Ogata proved in separate experiments that rat fleas were the key to plague's spread, almost nobody believed them. In 1899, the Indian Plague Commission reported on its extensive study of the disease. The Commission—a group of British and Indian researchers—completely discounted the two men's experiments. It claimed that other studies raised doubts about fleas transmitting plague.

Public health authorities around the world, including those in the United States, followed the Commission's advice on dealing with outbreaks. The best approach was to handle plague like other contagious diseases. Disinfect. Isolate. Quarantine.

HONOLULU HORROR

You Chong, a Chinese immigrant in his early twenties, had been living in the U.S. territory of Hawaii since 1898. He worked as a bookkeeper in a general store in Honolulu's Chinatown section. When You awoke on the morning of December 8, 1899, he knew something was wrong. He was burning with fever, and a painful swelling had appeared in his groin overnight.

His boss sent for a Chinese physician to help the young man. But You's case was hopeless. More swellings popped out under his armpits. He trembled violently, fell into a coma, and died within three days.

His doctor knew what these symptoms might mean. In an action that would later earn him the disdain of the Chinese community in Honolulu, the doctor reported the case to the Board of Health.

The Board sent three physicians, including a pathologist, to the store on Nuuanu Street where You's body lay. It looked like bubonic plague to them, too.

To be sure, they did an autopsy, and the pathologist took samples from the buboes and blood. When he checked them under a microscope, he saw what he believed were plague bacteria. He injected some into a rat and a guinea pig. The animals died from plague. By then, the Board of Health had heard of four other Chinatown residents who died with the same symptoms.

Plague had arrived in Hawaii, a place that never before had seen the disease.

The Board of Health's members—private citizens and government officials—were aware of the thousands of deaths in Hong Kong. In fact, they suspected that plague had arrived on ships from the colony. Determined to prevent the disease from spreading out of Chinatown into the rest of the city, the Board acted quickly.

The National Guard cordoned off the thirty-five acres of Honolulu's Chinese quarter. Going house to house, inspectors searched for victims and took the sick to a special hospital where they were

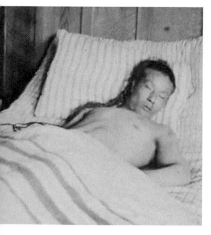

This Hawaiian man lies ill with plague during the 1900 outbreak.

56

Armed guards gather to enforce the quarantine of Honolulu's Chinatown.

isolated. People who had direct contact with the sick were forced into quarantine at two detention camps outside the city. Their belongings were disinfected and fumigated with chemicals.

About 10,000 people—mainly Chinese and Japanese immigrants—were quarantined within the cordon or at the camps. The Board of Health offered the Haffkine vaccine, and about 1,500 people asked for the injection. Some patients received the Yersin serum when they developed plague symptoms.

At the heart of the plague sanitation campaign was fire. Health inspectors condemned buildings where plague victims lived or worked. The fire department was directed to burn them down.

On Saturday morning, January 20, 1900, the department set fire to a wooden building in Chinatown. Unexpectedly, the wind shifted, blowing flames toward nearby structures.

Asians were allowed to leave Chinatown to work as servants for white employers. But before exiting the neighborhood, they were required to wash in a public disinfection station. Inspectors watch from the top of the fence to ensure that bathing is thorough.

Firefighters try to extinguish the out-of-control blaze in Chinatown, January 1900.

The tall twin steeples of the Kaumakapili Church caught fire. Firefighters couldn't spray water high enough to control the blaze. Strong gusts snatched the flames and drove them from one wooden building to another. In a warehouse, fireworks for the Chinese New Year exploded, worsening the inferno. Terrified residents ran for their lives.

By the time firefighters finally controlled the blaze, most of Chinatown was ashes. Miraculously, nobody died in the fire. As many as 6,000–8,000 people lost their homes, businesses, and everything they owned.

Tragically, plague wasn't wiped out. Hawaiian residents fell ill with painful buboes and high fevers for another two months. Some people in Honolulu realized that plague and rats were connected. They believed that the fire had driven rats to neighboring areas. But the Board of Health stayed focused on disinfection, quarantine, and fire.

The Honolulu plague outbreak didn't end until late March 1900. After disappearing from the city, the disease showed up on other Hawaiian islands later that year.

According to the official count, 71 people in Honolulu came down with plague, and 61 of them died. The majority of victims lived in or near Chinatown.

After winds shifted, fire consumed most of Chinatown's wooden structures.

Few buildings remained once the flames burned out.

Two years after the plague ended, the U.S. Congress paid $3 million to cover economic losses from the disease and fire. Chinatown residents weren't satisfied. They were convinced that the Hawaiian government intentionally let the fire burn out of control so that it would destroy their section of the city.

SLOWLY, SURELY

By the dawn of the twentieth century, plague had reached thirty countries on five continents and taken the lives of tens of thousands of people. Though scientists had found ways to help prevent plague and cure it, the vaccine and serum hadn't stopped the microbe from spreading and killing.

Surgeon General Walter Wyman was responsible for keeping infectious diseases out of the United States, and he was worried. In January 1900, he reported to his boss, the secretary of the treasury: "The epidemic is surely, though slowly, extending."

As he wrote his warning, the phantom killer was already on its way to America.

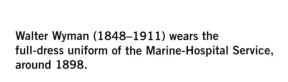

Walter Wyman (1848–1911) wears the full-dress uniform of the Marine-Hospital Service, around 1898.

THE UNITED STATES MARINE-HOSPITAL SERVICE

The Service began in 1798 when the U.S. Congress established hospitals to care for sick seamen. During the 1870s, the Service added to its mission the control of contagious diseases such as smallpox, cholera, and yellow fever.

The first surgeon general was appointed in 1871 to lead the organization.

The Service's Hygienic Laboratory was founded in 1887 to study diseases and their causes. Today, this research is carried out by the National Institutes of Health.

In the early 1890s, as millions of immigrants came to the United States, the Service took charge of protecting the country from imported infectious diseases. Medical officers checked all ships entering American ports from other countries. If they found any obvious signs of a contagious disease, they ordered the ship and its contents to be disinfected, steamed, or fumigated. Service officers had the authority to quarantine passengers and crew until doctors made sure that no one was sick and carrying disease. Those diagnosed with a contagious illness were kept in isolation.

In 1902, the Service's name changed to the Public Health and Marine-Hospital Service. Ten years later, it became the Public Health Service, the name used today. The PHS is now part of the Department of Health and Human Services.

CHAPTER SEVEN

DEATH IN CHINATOWN

"The existence of plague in San Francisco is a matter of great seriousness."

—Wilfred Kellogg, 1900

O n Tuesday, March 6, 1900, a laborer from Canton, China, lay dying in the dank basement of the run-down Globe Hotel in San Francisco's Chinatown. For more than two weeks, Wong Chut King* had been too sick to show up for work at a lumberyard on Pacific Street. He burned with fever. Every muscle ached. He vomited and had diarrhea. After becoming delirious, Wong fell into a coma.

His roommates in the crowded rooming house considered it bad luck—and even dangerous—to be near someone when he died. So they lifted Wong from his narrow bunk and carried him a few blocks to a Chinese undertaker, or coffin shop. That evening, Wong breathed his last.

[*Variously called Chick Gin, Cheek Gun, Wing Chit King, or Wing Chung Ging by the local newspapers and health authorities at the time.]

San Francisco's Market Street is busy with cable cars, horse-drawn carts, and pedestrians, around 1899.

Because no one knew why he died, the police were called. A police surgeon, Frank Wilson, came to the coffin shop to examine the body. It was his responsibility to investigate suspicious deaths.

In the dim light of the shop, Wilson checked the body of the forty-one-year-old Wong. He noticed an unusual dark swelling in the man's right groin. With the recent news from Honolulu on his mind, Wilson ran his hand over it. Could this be a bubo? Not wanting to take any chances, he sent for the city's health officer, A. P. O'Brien.

After examining Wong's body, O'Brien agreed. Both doctors were unnerved by the possibility that plague had shown up in San Francisco. O'Brien asked the police to quarantine Wong's rooming house until he knew more.

Next, O'Brien called the health department's bacteriologist, Wilfred Kellogg. Later that night, Kellogg cut out some of Wong's swollen lymph nodes. When he looked at fluid from the nodes under the microscope, he spotted tiny oval organisms. This wasn't good, he told O'Brien. The microbes were probably plague bacteria.

Yet the bacteriologist remained cautious. "I have reason to suspect that Cheek Gun [Wong] died of bubonic plague," he later announced to the press. "Still, my examination has not progressed sufficiently to warrant a positive statement to that effect." More tests would have to be done, he said, to confirm that the microbes from Wong's body were plague bacteria. Results might take several days.

O'Brien couldn't wait. He'd read the reports from Bombay the previous September when more than 4,000 people died of plague in one week. As health officer, he wouldn't let that happen in San Francisco.

THE CHINATOWN "FEEDING GROUND"

Chinatown was twelve blocks of crowded streets and run-down buildings jammed together not far from the wharves. Dark basement passageways and narrow alleys connected homes and businesses.

Pipes led to open sewers, which backed up and drained into basements when it rained, creating a foul stench. Landlords made no attempt to improve the unsanitary living conditions.

Wong was like the majority of Chinatown residents—unmarried men working long hours at low-paying jobs and sending money back to their families in China. Stringent immigration laws made it illegal for a Chinese laborer to marry in the United States or to bring a wife from China. To save on expenses, several men typically crowded into a single dark, airless, filthy room like the one where Wong had a bunk.

A Chinatown street in the 1890s. Living quarters were often cramped and unsanitary, but most people had enough money to buy adequate food and clothing.

The majority of Chinatown residents in 1900 were unmarried men.

O'Brien considered Chinatown "a magnificent feeding ground" for plague. How many other people in the maze of streets and buildings were harboring plague bacteria? Was Wong just the first to die?

O'Brien and the San Francisco Board of Health decided to act immediately to stop the disease from spreading. Unaware of the flea experiments by Simond and Ogata, O'Brien and other city health experts assumed that plague was contagious between people. They would combat the disease the same way as the public health officials did in Hong Kong, Bombay, and Honolulu.

The next day, as a light rain fell during the early morning darkness, police officers strung ropes across all intersections leading into Chinatown. Guards allowed no one to enter and only whites to exit through the blockade.

A cartoon from the *San Francisco Call* shows a police officer rounding up a Chinatown resident who tried to escape the area's cordon.

Most of the 10,000 to 15,000 residents inside Chinatown's cordon didn't realize what had happened until daybreak. Workers complained to the guards that they needed to get out to their jobs in other parts of the city. The police turned them back. Food deliveries were halted. Garbage collection stopped, leaving piles of rubbish on the street. Street cars were forbidden to pass through the area. Later Wednesday morning, the Board of Health sent in inspectors to search for other plague victims.

Using formaldehyde as a disinfectant, workers washed down Wong's room and the coffin shop where he died. They took his bedding and clothes into the street and burned them. On the buildings' doors, inspectors tacked signs in English and Chinese announcing that a death from plague had occurred inside.

The health authorities were more

interested in stemming the spread of plague than in offending foreign customs. Chinese tradition forbade cutting a corpse. It opposed cremation because "the ashes will be scattered in the air and let go to the home of nothingness, the cave of emptiness." Customarily, the bones of the dead were sent back to China for proper burial.

Nevertheless, Kellogg had sliced out Wong's swollen lymph nodes. A horse-drawn cart later took the man's body to a cemetery where it, like his belongings, was burned.

THE MAN ON ANGEL ISLAND

That afternoon, while police guarded the perimeter of Chinatown, the health department's bacteriologist set out on a journey. Carefully carrying samples from Wong's lymph glands in a jar of alcohol, Wilfred Kellogg sat aboard a ferryboat crossing the San Francisco Bay.

A half hour later, he stepped onto Angel Island, where the U.S. Marine-Hospital Service maintained its quarantine station and sophisticated bacteriology laboratory. Walking into the lab, Kellogg handed the samples to Joseph Kinyoun, the chief quarantine officer.

Was he correct, Kellogg asked, when he identified plague bacteria the previous night?

Kinyoun was aware that Chinatown had been quarantined. Now it would be up to him to determine whether plague killed the man. As one of the country's most skilled bacteriologists, Kinyoun was up to the challenge.

Born in North Carolina in 1860 and raised in Missouri, he began studying medicine with his physician father at age sixteen. Later, Kinyoun went to New York City for formal training at Bellevue Medical College, earning his medical degree in 1882.

When he was offered an opportunity to enroll in Bellevue's

Joseph Kinyoun (1860–1919) directed the Hygienic Laboratory from 1887 to 1899. It later grew into today's National Institutes of Health.

new bacteriology program, he took it. The discoveries of Koch and Pasteur had created this new scientific field, and Kinyoun was hungry to learn all he could about disease-causing microbes.

In October 1886, after finishing the program, the twenty-six-year-old Kinyoun joined the Marine-Hospital Service. He was assigned to set up the Service's first bacteriology research facility, called the Hygienic Laboratory, at the quarantine station on Staten Island, New York. His job was to study contagious diseases, including smallpox and yellow fever, and examine samples from sick ship passengers to find out what diseases they carried.

Just a month after his one-room laboratory opened, Kinyoun identified cholera bacteria in passengers on two Italian ships. His finding came in time to isolate the sick and avert an epidemic in New York City. It was the first time in America that bacteriology had been used to confirm cholera among arriving immigrants.

The Service later sent Kinyoun to Europe where he studied bacteriology with Koch, Kitasato, Pasteur, and Roux. During a trip in 1894, he learned the laboratory techniques for identifying the newly discovered plague bacterium.

When Kinyoun returned to the Hygienic Laboratory, he brought back the latest techniques for producing serums and vaccines. One was an antitoxin against diphtheria, the same disease that had killed his three-year-old daughter several years before.

ASIAN THREAT

By 1899, Surgeon General Walter Wyman had become increasingly concerned about San Francisco. Of all the U.S. ports, it received the most ship traffic from Asia, where cholera and plague were serious problems. He wanted an officer at the quarantine station who was experienced in bacteriology. Kinyoun was the man. Wyman knew him well, having been his immediate supervisor when Kinyoun first set up the Hygienic Laboratory.

Late that spring, Kinyoun assumed command, moving his pregnant wife and three children to the house on Angel Island. He wasn't happy about being there. The work was important, certainly. But others could do it. Kinyoun was capable of so much more. He couldn't help feeling that this assignment was a waste of his talents.

From the time he arrived, Kinyoun had been watching for plague. He knew it was only a matter of time before the disease struck. With a population of 343,000 people, San Francisco was California's largest city and the ninth most populated in the country. The city was similar to others in the world already infected. It was a major port visited by ships from all over the globe. And it also had crowded neighborhoods of poor immigrants living in unsanitary conditions.

Following the Service's guidelines, Kinyoun required all vessels coming from ports where plague had been found—Hong Kong; Honolulu; Kobe, Japan; Sydney, Australia—to fly a yellow flag as they entered the harbor. This signaled that the ship must be put in quarantine until cleared by the Service.

U.S. ports had already had a few close calls. In November 1899, a British ship arrived in New York City from Brazil. A steward on the ship had fallen ill during the journey and died at sea. Next, the ship's captain and cook became sick. By the time they arrived in New York, the two were recovering.

Marine-Hospital Service inspectors discovered a bubo in each man's groin. When they examined the pus inside, they found *Yersinia pestis*. The Service quarantined the ship and its crew. Nobody else fell ill, and plague stayed out of New York City.

Beginning in the late 1800s, authorities throughout the world inspected ships and their crews for plague. The man raises his arms as a medical officer checks for buboes in his armpits.

Then, in late January 1900, a Japanese ship arrived at Port Townsend, Washington, with a sick passenger showing enlarged lymph glands. The man later died at the quarantine station. The Service doctor suspected plague, and he quarantined the boat and its other passengers until laboratory results came back. Tests confirmed the doctor's suspicions. Eventually, 17 people from the ship developed the disease, and 3 died. Since all had been held in quarantine, plague never spread from the ship.

Before Wong Chut King's death, San Francisco had its own plague scare in June 1899 from a Japanese ship sailing from Hong Kong. During the vessel's voyage, two people died of plague. Following procedure for ships with a recent history of the disease, the Service quarantined the vessel at Angel Island. None of the passengers and crew showed plague symptoms, but they weren't allowed to disembark in the city.

When Service officers inspected the ship, they discovered eleven Japanese stowaways. The next day, two of the stowaways were missing. Later, local authorities found the men floating dead in San Francisco Bay, still wearing life preservers from the ship.

Recent arrivals wait to disembark at the U.S. Quarantine Station on Angel Island in 1896. They had been transferred to this boat from the ship that brought them from China.

The city's health department investigated and believed it found plague bacteria in the two stowaways' bodies. Kinyoun wasn't convinced. He hadn't examined the bodies himself, and he didn't trust the department's lab work.

Nobody from the ship developed plague, but Kinyoun worried that the next time San Francisco wouldn't be so lucky. Somehow plague would get off a ship and invade the city. Was the body in Chinatown the first sign that it already had?

To confirm that the bacteria in Wong's lymph glands were plague, Kinyoun used the standard process. He injected material from the glands into two guinea pigs, a white rat, and a monkey. If the test animals died with plague symptoms, such as swollen glands, he'd check samples from their bodies under the microscope.

Kinyoun and the rest of San Francisco would have to wait three or four days to see what happened.

WHERE'S THE PROOF?

Meanwhile, tensions were rising in Chinatown. To the Chinese, the quarantine seemed like another example of the discrimination they'd endured for years. Ever since Chinese immigrants arrived in California in the early 1850s to mine gold, laws treated them differently. They were forced to live by special rules when it came to working, owning businesses, paying taxes, marrying, and becoming American citizens.

Over the following decades, more immigrants arrived to build railroads; work in factories, shops, and on farms;

In the 1800s, many Americans did not welcome Chinese immigrants. The 1882 cartoon caption reads: "The Only One Barred Out. Enlightened American Statesman.—'We must draw the line *somewhere*, you know.'"

FRANK LESLIE'S ILLUSTRATED NEWSPAPER.

THE ONLY ONE BARRED OUT.
ENLIGHTENED AMERICAN STATESMAN.—" We must draw the line *somewhere*, you know."

The October 1880 riot in Denver, Colorado. Incited by anti-Chinese politicians and the press, a mob of three thousand Denverites attacked Chinese residents and destroyed their homes and businesses. One man was beaten to death.

and become servants and cooks. Wong Chut King was one of many who traveled to California from small farming villages near Canton, China.

Some Americans resented the newcomers for taking jobs from white men. Others considered Asians an inferior race that had poor hygiene and, as a result, spread disease. Starting in the 1880s, new laws severely restricted Chinese immigration. Throughout the United States, including San Francisco, the Chinese often became victims of violence.

By March 1900, people in Chinatown had read what happened in Honolulu a few weeks before. If it turned out that Wong died of plague, would their homes be torched, too?

The Chinese government's consul general in San Francisco, Ho Yow, had plenty to say about the quarantine. In official flyers posted around Chinatown, he threatened his government's retaliation for the "outrageous conduct" against people from his country.

The Chinese Six Companies, a group representing and assisting immigrants, charged that the blockade hurt business in Chinatown. Furthermore, it claimed that Wong had lived in the city for more than fifteen years. How could he have been infected if no one in America had plague? The swelling in his groin, the group said, was likely caused by a sexually transmitted disease Wong had had for six months.

Several Chinese leaders confronted the Board of Health, demanding that it "remove the ban they have placed upon us." If the Board refused, they planned to ask the courts to lift the quarantine.

The Chinese weren't the only ones who were angry. San Francisco businesses, hotels, and families that depended on Chinese workers wanted their employees released from the blockade. White businessmen

Chinatown residents quarantined during the plague outbreak, from *Harper's Weekly*, June 2, 1900

complained that visitors would be frightened away by the quarantine, costing the city tourist money. The world would think that San Francisco was infected with plague. Where was the proof of that?

THE PRESS ATTACKS

The city's newspapers criticized the quarantine as "a sham of the flimsiest kind." Everyone knew that people were escaping from Chinatown through alleys and underground passages or by climbing on roofs.

One newspaper charged that "the purpose of the quarantine was more for the purpose of keeping the Chinese than the plague in Chinatown."

Another condemned the Board of Health for its "sensational statement . . . that there was a case of the dread disease in Chinatown." The article went on to say, "The bubonic plague fake" was part of a plan to get more city funds directed to the Board and to the mayor's friends. "The most dangerous plague which threatens San Francisco is not of the bubonic type." It was "a plague of politics."

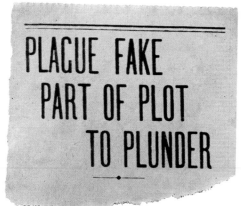

Headlines from the *San Francisco Call*, March 8 (above) and March 9 (right), 1900

An editorial charged that the whole affair was "a scientific farce" and that the Board of Health relied "on the testimony of a rat, a monkey and a guinea-pig." Kinyoun's animals would

probably die from the illness that killed the Chinese victim, the editorial said, but that illness was certainly not plague.

The public reaction inside and outside Chinatown was too much for San Francisco's health authorities. Kinyoun hadn't yet confirmed that the dead man had plague. Without that, they were forced to give in to the pressure.

74

PLAGUE FARCE IS OVER AND HEALTH BOARD QUITS THE STAGE

On Friday, March 9, the Board of Health lifted the Chinatown quarantine. Out of caution, it required all suspicious disease cases in Chinatown to be reported. Not trusting Chinese doctors to follow this decree, the city sent thirty inspectors to check every house for plague victims. The Board also ordered residents and businesses to clean up their property with disinfectants.

Chinese consul Ho Yow repeated his warning about the quarantine. If it happened again, there would be "international consequence."

While the newspapers attacked the Board of Health and the Six Companies threatened lawsuits, Joseph Kinyoun watched his animals on Angel Island. Were the bacteria taken from Wong's body really plague?

Two days after the quarantine was lifted, he had his answer.

From the *San Francisco Call*, March 10, 1900, the day after the Board of Health lifted the Chinatown quarantine

MARCH 11, 1900.

CHINATOWN WILL BE TREATED TO A GENERAL BATH

Board of Health Now Trying to Redeem Itself Before the Public.

End of the Quarantine Fizzle Finally Allows the Chinese to Resume Business and Be Reasonably Happy.

The *San Francisco Call* celebrates the end of the Chinatown quarantine and announces the disinfecting campaign.

CHAPTER EIGHT

THE MONKEY DIED

"An epidemic is like a conflagration—it is most easily suppressed at the beginning."

—*Walter Wyman, 1900*

When Kinyoun checked his test animals on Sunday, March 11, 1900, he found the lifeless bodies of the rat and two guinea pigs in their cages. Two days later, the monkey died.

Kinyoun carefully examined the bodies. Each animal had swollen lymph nodes and spleen. Samples from their spleens and blood contained the oval plague bacteria.

This was the proof Kinyoun needed. He sent Surgeon General Wyman a short telegram with the bad news: "Completed examination. Specimens [from] dead Chinese demonstrate plague."

The killer had attacked its first victim on North American soil.

How did the microbes get here? Kinyoun had his suspicions. Probably by a ship entering the port from one of the Asian plague areas. An infected passenger, rat, or cargo had made it to shore despite efforts to inspect, disinfect, and quarantine ships.

Kinyoun couldn't help wondering if Wong was really the first victim. Few physicians, including those in Chinatown, had ever seen plague. Bubonic cases were hard to spot if the infected lymph nodes weren't large. Pneumonic and septicemic were even more difficult to diagnose. Had there been other unexplained deaths never investigated by the health department? No one would ever know.

OFFICIAL ADVICE

Walter Wyman wasn't surprised by Kinyoun's report. He had anticipated this day, and he'd been getting ready.

Wyman had been with the Marine-Hospital Service since 1876. After growing up in St. Louis, Missouri, and earning his medical degree from St. Louis Medical College, he decided to pursue a career in public health. Ambitious and politically savvy, Wyman rapidly advanced in the Service. In 1891, President Benjamin Harrison appointed the forty-two-year-old doctor to be surgeon general.

Wyman led the Service as it grew in size and responsibility. He improved ship inspections, expanded federal control of quarantines, and increased research into infectious diseases. A bachelor, Wyman dedicated all his time to the Service, supervising every detail of its operations, including the military style of the uniforms its medical officers wore. He kept in close touch with his officers stationed throughout the United States and the world, personally responding to their letters and telegrams.

When the Third Pandemic began, in China, Wyman prepared his officers. He kept them informed about plague's spread. At his direction, some of them attended the international plague conference in Italy and studied with scientists at the Pasteur Institute.

As soon as Wyman received word that a man had died in Chinatown, very possibly from plague, he wired a telegram to the

Service officers in San Francisco. "Make following suggestions to local board of health: All inhabitants of Chinatown to be treated with the Haffkine [vaccine] or [Yersin] serum." Wyman immediately sent thousands of doses of both from Washington, D.C., a supply "sufficient for a good beginning."

CHINESE SCATTER TO AVOID A THREATENED QUARANTINE

Health Board Meets and Adopts Measures to Cleanse the Mongolian Quarter of All Sorts of Bacilli.

Headline from the *San Francisco Call*, March 13, 1900. Kinyoun's test results alarmed health officials. The Chinese feared another quarantine.

Even though the Marine-Hospital Service and San Francisco's health officials were convinced by Kinyoun's lab results, many others refused to believe that Wong died of plague.

The *Pacific Medical Journal* was critical of Kinyoun's report. "There is not in the city a case of Bubonic plague, and . . . there has never been any good reason for quarantining even a portion of the city."

Ho Yow used strong language to object. He called the claim "a ruse on the part of the board of health" to justify "the outrageous acts of last week in quarantining the Chinese quarter." Of course, he would do everything in his power to protect people in the city if there really was plague. But Ho told the Board not to attempt a Chinatown blockade again.

MORE DEATHS

On Thursday, March 15, health officials received word of a death in a room on Sacramento Street, several blocks from where Wong had lived. The decomposed body looked as if the man had been dead for a week. His face was swollen, and he had blister-like marks on his greenish-black skin. He had no buboes, though his spleen was enlarged.

According to people who knew the Chinese laborer, twenty-two-year-old Chew Gam had been sick for at least a month. The health department didn't trust that information. Bacteriologist

A toy peddler on a Chinatown street around 1900. Despite reports of plague, most people in Chinatown didn't believe it.

Wilfred Kellogg examined the man's blood under his microscope. He saw microbes that he thought could be plague.

Two days later, another decomposed body of a young Chinese man showed up at a coffin shop. Ng Ach Ging's body contained no buboes either.

A third rotting male body was found on March 18. Lee Sung Kong had been dead two days, and like the other two men, he had no buboes.

The health department had avoided performing complete autopsies, knowing this would upset the Chinese. But these three deaths raised an alarm. The department's doctors decided to cut open the bodies.

They invited Kinyoun to assist with the autopsies. From the appearance of the organs, he suspected plague. He took samples from the blood and spleen of each man. Back on Angel Island, he injected the specimens into test animals.

Within thirty-six hours, the animals were dead. When Kinyoun checked their bodies for bacteria, he saw an "organism very suspicious." The three men had apparently died from septicemic, not bubonic, plague. Their deaths proved to Kinyoun that Wong Chut King had not been an isolated case.

The plague epidemics during the six years since Canton had all started slowly, with a few sporadic, often unrelated cases. Then the outbreak exploded. Kinyoun sent an urgent telegram to Wyman in Washington: "Expect there will be further spread. Every condition favorable among this population. Requires quick action. No time to lose."

CLEANUP

John Williamson, president of the San Francisco Board of Health, was worried, too. Could the city expect an out-of-control epidemic like the ones in Hong Kong and Bombay?

Tensions were too high to attempt another quarantine. Instead, Williamson begged the mayor and the city's board of supervisors for more money to sanitize Chinatown. The health department didn't even have the funds to pay the thirty inspectors now on duty, he told them. And despite pleas to one hundred local physicians, only ten volunteered to help. "There is no use evading the issue," said Williamson. "The Chinese quarter of this city is infected with plague."

The city's leaders took Williamson's concerns seriously. On March 21, they voted to give the health department $7,500 to pay 30 doctors and 120 inspectors.

"The whole neighborhood [will be] drenched with disinfectants," Williamson promised.

The cartoon in the *San Francisco Call*, March 13, 1900, reflects attitudes about plague and the city's Chinese population.

The sanitary team pushed their way into homes and forced people to clean up living quarters and businesses. Get rid of dust, insects, and rodents, inspectors instructed residents, because those can carry plague bacteria. Wash the walls, floors, and furniture with disinfectant.

City crews cleared trash from streets and buildings, then hauled away the rubbish. Workers fumigated sewers every day with germ-killing gas, creating clouds of stinking yellow sulfur that seeped from the manholes. They spread tons of bleaching powder

A store in a Chinatown alley around 1900. Chickens hang from a rack, and fish lie on the tables.

on yards and streets until the neighborhood looked as though snow had fallen.

The health department didn't stop there. The recent victims had all been dead a couple of days before city authorities found them. It was obvious that Chinatown's residents were hiding bodies and sending the sick out of the city.

Using its added manpower, the department checked every house and shop in Chinatown each day for plague victims. It stationed inspectors at railroad stations and ferries to examine Asians who tried to leave the city. They detained for testing anyone who seemed sick. Dozens of policemen backed up the inspectors in case of trouble.

Meanwhile, on Angel Island, Kinyoun and his Service inspectors focused on the federal government's responsibility: scrutinizing ships, their passengers, and their cargo coming *into* San Francisco, especially from plague-infected ports.

THE WORD GETS OUT

San Francisco's business community wanted the new plague cases to remain a secret. It couldn't afford to have the entire nation and world view the city as a disease hotspot. What would happen to trade if ships refused to dock in San Francisco?

Most of the city's newspapers kept the secret by reporting that there was no plague or that it had faded away. The *San Francisco Call* made fun of Kinyoun's lab results and the health department's inspectors poking around Chinatown's maze of alleyways:

"Health Board, Health Board,
Where are we at?
Guinea pig, guinea pig,
Rat, rat, rat!"

But the news had already leaked out. The *San Francisco Examiner* and its sister newspaper the *New York Journal* ran sensational

headlines such as "The Black Plague Creeps Into San Francisco."
The businessmen's fears came true when other papers around the
country picked up the stories. The *Denver Republican* announced:
"Tourists Fleeing from Plague Stricken San Francisco."

San Francisco's leaders hoped the city could weather the storm.
In early April, they proudly announced that no new plague victims
had been found. The bacteria were gone. The month-long sanitation
campaign had been a success.

FIVE MORE

They were wrong.

On Tuesday night, April 24, thirty-eight-year-old Law An died
in Chinatown with a large bubo in his left groin. When Kinyoun
injected two guinea pigs with samples from the swelling, both
animals died of plague within three days.

By the third week in May 1900, four more people succumbed to
bubonic plague, including two sixteen-year-old girls.

The new cases distressed Kinyoun. He wired Surgeon General
Wyman: It "will require almost superhuman efforts to control now,
so much time has been lost."

Kinyoun thought their best chance of avoiding a full-scale
epidemic was to give the Haffkine vaccine to San Francisco's
entire Asian population, the most vulnerable. "Over 35,000 people
must be controlled," he wrote. Health authorities might even have
to resort to "depopulation" by moving people out of Chinatown.
Kinyoun's idea was to hold them in a detention camp on an island
in the bay until another cleanup operation was finished.

Back in Washington, Wyman responded to the crisis quickly.
He ordered additional Service officers to San Francisco from their
posts in other parts of the country. He sent more Haffkine vaccine
so that there would be enough to inoculate the Chinatown
population if necessary.

Wyman told Kinyoun to advise local health officials to reinstate the quarantine and disinfection. He strongly recommended that the city set up a pesthouse in Chinatown or on Angel Island where suspected plague cases would be taken and isolated.

Although Wyman and Kinyoun gave advice to San Francisco's leaders, the federal Marine-Hospital Service didn't have the power to dictate how the city handled disease within its own borders. The only actions the Service could take at the moment were to monitor the port, assist with bacteriological tests, and make the vaccine available.

A wealthy Chinese businessman and his sons walking in Chinatown, around 1900. Many residents resented the health department's actions.

TIME FOR HAFFKINE

The city's leaders recognized that the recent deaths meant they could be facing a major epidemic. On May 18, 1900, the San Francisco Board of Health formally declared that plague existed in the city and that health department personnel would respond right away.

Newspapers throughout the country informed their readers of the latest developments: "Bubonic Horror at San Francisco"; "Dread Plague."

The day after the Board's announcement, the city's health department doctors and inspectors converged on Chinatown again. This time the sanitary team took along the Haffkine vaccine to inoculate anyone who wanted it.

Most residents were too afraid to get the injection. They'd heard rumors that whites were trying to poison them. Signs posted around Chinatown announced that the dangerous shot had already killed people. Besides, why was the city trying to give them a vaccine when there was no plague?

Many Chinese believed that if anybody *had* died of plague in Chinatown, it was because the public health authorities planted the disease there. Others thought the dead victims had been sickened with the disinfection chemicals and fumes.

Inspectors resumed their door-to-door sanitation checks, but the people of Chinatown had had enough. Mobs attacked the inspectors on their rounds. In one incident, two men hit a health inspector with bricks and bats when they saw him checking a well. They assumed he was poisoning the water.

Chinatown residents barricaded their doors and shuttered their windows. They closed their stores and restaurants. People huddled inside, fearful that they'd be sent away to a pesthouse or an island in the bay, even for a minor ailment. They didn't want to be forced from their home and have all their belongings burned. Those who could afford to hire transportation out of the city sent their families elsewhere. Streets were nearly empty.

ALL A SHAM

Most San Franciscans thought that the plague talk was baseless. Local newspapers had convinced them that "there has been and is no bubonic plague in San Francisco." If the disease was really in Chinatown, why hadn't more people died, the way they did in other countries?

Reporters quoted physicians who blamed the Chinatown deaths on other infectious illnesses such as typhoid fever, pneumonia, and venereal disease. According to these doctors, Kinyoun's test animals likely died from injections of one of those microbes.

Some critics suggested that, as part of a deception, tissues supposedly taken from victims were deliberately contaminated with plague bacteria.

According to the press, the entire affair was a sham. The health department and Kinyoun had failed to show one bit of evidence that plague caused these deaths. "Can you, Dr. Kinyoun, perform any greater service than the annihilation of a menagerie at your Federal quarantine station?" asked one newspaper. The result of this lie was "a well developed panic outside of San Francisco" that had ruined business and trade.

Kinyoun was disgusted by the news coverage. Nine San Francisco residents had died of plague, and the public didn't care. He told Wyman in a telegram, "People here [are] absolutely in dark as to correct situation."

CAN ANY ONE TELL WHO INSPIRED THE RAID?

Some newspapers claimed that corrupt city officials invented the plague scare to enrich their friends with taxpayer money. This cartoon from the *San Francisco Call*, March 20, 1900, uses Kinyoun's three test animals to make that point.

CONTAIN THEM

Kinyoun realized that the health department's anti-plague campaign wasn't working. "In my opinion," he wired Wyman, "[it] will require a regiment before any good will be done."

He and Wyman had to take a broader view. What if people, frightened or angered by the renewed inspections, left the state? They might carry plague bacteria and start an epidemic that could sweep the country. The Service already had the legal authority to use quarantines on people traveling into the United States and across state lines. Kinyoun and Wyman wanted to use it.

Wyman obtained permission from President William McKinley to ban travel by Asians coming from a plague area—San Francisco—

unless they showed proof of inoculation. He instructed his officers, "Allow no Chinese or Japanese to pass out without certificate from Marine-Hospital Service."

As the federal quarantine officer, Kinyoun ordered San Francisco transportation companies not to sell tickets to Asians unless they had this proof. Marine-Hospital officers inspected trains, ferries, and ships at exit points from the city and at key state border crossings. On the spot, officers offered the Haffkine vaccine to travelers. They had few takers.

Japan's government complained to the U.S. State Department that the action discriminated against Japanese residents of the city. People, including a member of Japan's parliament, had "been treated with great indignity" and ladies were "rudely seized."

The Chinese, too, were angered by the renewed inspections, the inoculations, and the travel restrictions. The Chinese minister complained to the U.S. secretary of state. Consul Ho Yow made new accusations: "The health board would not dare to treat any other race this way."

In San Francisco, a Chinatown crowd demanded that their representatives protect them. On May 24, the Six Companies' attorneys filed a lawsuit in U.S. Circuit Court challenging the ban on travel out of the city by Chinese who wouldn't agree to be vaccinated.

The suit charged that the Board of Health and the federal quarantine officer, Kinyoun, had prohibited Chinese merchant Wong Wai from leaving the city to travel within California to conduct his business. This travel restriction discriminated against Wong as well as "the 25,000 persons of the Chinese race" living in San Francisco.

"There is not now and never has been any case of bubonic plague" in the city, the lawyers argued. They asked the federal judge to end the Haffkine inoculations and the ban on travel out of the city.

Four days later, Judge William Morrow agreed to stop both. In his decision, he said that the travel regulation was enforced against only one specific group—Asians. The U.S. Constitution's Fourteenth Amendment guaranteed that all people are protected equally by laws. One race cannot be singled out for different treatment. Therefore, the travel ban on Asians leaving the city for other parts of California was unconstitutional. And Chinese residents could not be required to be inoculated if they didn't want to be.

For Kinyoun, Morrow's decision was a disaster. Now, he expected, "a large exodus [of] Chinese and Japanese will begin to surrounding country and States." He knew that plague bacteria were in Chinatown. Fewer than 900 people in San Francisco had received the Haffkine vaccine. He was convinced that the "situation to United States [was] very grave."

The ban on travel from San Francisco was aimed at Asians. White travelers were not considered to be at risk of carrying plague. This photograph was taken at a California train station in 1905.

CHAPTER NINE

QUARANTINE OUTRAGE

"It is unreasonable, unjust, and oppressive."

—Judge William Morrow, 1900

The judge had stopped the inoculations and the travel restrictions. But city leaders couldn't afford to abandon the anti-plague efforts. Several states threatened to bar passengers and cargo coming from San Francisco and California. The city had to show that plague was under control.

On May 28, 1900, the San Francisco Board of Supervisors declared that plague existed, putting the city on firmer legal ground than it had been with the Board of Health's May 18 declaration. The Supervisors voted to authorize a quarantine "necessary to prevent the spreading of contagious or infectious diseases" in the city.

The next day, the second quarantine of Chinatown began. More than 150 police officers guarded the roped-off perimeter. This time, health officials added barbed-wire barricades on some streets.

Inspectors renewed their search for plague victims, with the

Ropes and barbed wire block off Chinatown during the second quarantine in late May 1900.

intention of moving them into isolation. The health department resumed the Chinatown cleanup. The district was "a menace to public health," the city's chief sanitary inspector proclaimed. He blamed the dirty conditions on the "aliens, who differ in their customs, habits and ideas of sanitation from those approved by modern sanitarians."

Kinyoun was concerned that the city was missing one key element in their campaign: rat-killing. The Service considered rats "without doubt . . . the most active agents of spreading [bubonic plague]." The cleanup would help lower the rat population because the rodents found food and shelter in the filth. But to stop the plague outbreak, Kinyoun told the Board of Health, the city had to eradicate them.

On Angel Island, he said, the Service used sulfur dioxide gas to kill rodents aboard incoming ships, and the city should use it, too. Kinyoun also recommended traps and poison bait, such as fish stuffed with arsenic.

Acting on his suggestion, the Boards of Health and Public Works began a rat destruction campaign in Chinatown and nearby neighborhoods. Unfortunately, the city lacked the money to carry on the kind of extensive rat-killing plan that Kinyoun advised.

NO PLAGUE HERE

Among Chinatown residents, the second quarantine was even less popular than the first. Consul Ho Yow charged that health authorities had put people living inside the cordon at risk. "Do they want to imprison the residents of the entire district and force them to contract the plague?"

The *San Francisco Call* pointed out that the blockade wouldn't stop an epidemic from spreading—if there actually was one. "No white man can enter, but any white man can come out;

The cordon was supposed to prevent plague's spread from people inside Chinatown to other San Franciscans. Yet it didn't stop these Chinese and white men from carrying on a face-to-face conversation across the rope.

no Chinaman can come out, but any Chinaman can enter." People stood on either side of the barrier, the paper said, talking and passing packages back and forth. "That is the sort of thing which is called 'quarantining against the bubonic plague.'"

The day the *Call*'s critical article appeared, Dang Hong died in a coffin shop on Pacific Street in Chinatown. His lymph nodes were filled with plague bacteria.

During the next fourteen days, 2 more men died of plague. By early June, the outbreak had claimed a total of 12 lives in Chinatown. Kinyoun wondered if other victims had been hidden from health officials or smuggled out of the city.

Once again, San Francisco's Chinese population and most of the press refused to believe that the latest deaths were from plague. Newspapers quoted physicians who said that nobody had yet died of the disease. Kinyoun heard rumors that some newspapers were paying for medical opinions that refuted his lab-test results and the health department's diagnoses.

California's governor, Henry T. Gage, publicly questioned plague's existence, too. He objected to meddling by the Marine-Hospital Service into the affairs of the state. And he didn't like the actions of the San Francisco Board of Health, either.

In a telegram to the U.S. secretary of state, Gage declared, "Bubonic plague does not exist and has not existed within the State of California." He claimed to have talked to plague experts who witnessed the disease in India, and they assured him that the dead were not plague victims.

BURN IT DOWN!

But as more deaths occurred, other people became convinced that the city had to do something about Chinatown—immediately. If there wasn't plague now, other diseases certainly could breed there. Such a foul slum, right in the heart of the city, was a disgrace.

A man delivers supplies into Chinatown by pushing them under the cordon rope.

It was bad for business if San Francisco was considered a dirty place, harboring such "appalling disgustfulness." A member of the state board of health announced, "I would advocate the complete destruction of Chinatown by fire."

San Francisco's Chinese newspapers reported on the calls to level Chinatown and on the city's plans to set up detention centers for everyone exposed to plague. Anxiety rose in the neighborhood.

On June 5, the Six Companies threatened that if anyone was removed from Chinatown, the Chinese would resist by force. Lawyers for the group filed a lawsuit on behalf of Jew Ho, who owned a grocery store on the edge of Chinatown, and the thousands of people caught inside the cordon.

The suit charged that the quarantine discriminated against Jew. The barricade curved to include his grocery but not neighboring white-owned businesses. None of his customers from outside the cordon could reach his store. The quarantine was unnecessary since there "never has been any case of bubonic plague."

Ten days later, Judge Morrow announced his decision to a crowded courtroom of lawyers, press, and spectators. The quarantine, he said, "is made to operate against the Chinese population only, and the reason given for it is that the Chinese may communicate the disease from one to the other." That makes it discrimination against Asians. "It is unreasonable, unjust, and oppressive," Morrow continued, "and therefore contrary to the laws limiting the police powers of the State and municipality."

He ordered Chinatown's cordon removed. The Board of Health could not quarantine an entire section of the city. Morrow allowed health officials to quarantine and disinfect only individual houses where they found infected people.

By midafternoon, police officers took down the ropes and barbed wire. After nearly three weeks, the second quarantine of Chinatown was over.

Shopkeepers opened their stores. Delivery wagons resumed

their rounds in the neighborhood. People once again appeared on the streets, hurrying in and out of Chinatown and trying to return to their normal routine. Many had been afraid that the health department would yank them from their homes and burn their community to the ground. Judge Morrow erased their fears.

BACK TO COURT

The quarantine was over, but Kinyoun's problems were not. He still had a duty to prevent plague from spreading *out* of California. Morrow's ruling concerned travel within the state. Kinyoun believed the Service had the legal power to forbid people from leaving for

CALIFORNIA IS SUBJECTED TO AN UNPARALLELED OUTRAGE

Dr. J. J. Kinyoun Strikes a Serious Blow to the State by Arbitrarily and Without Cause Placing It Under Federal Quarantine.

The headlines and cartoons from the *San Francisco Call*, June 17, 1900, reveal the newspaper's critical opinion of Kinyoun's travel ban.

Incidents in the Outrage of the State Quarantine.

other states if they lacked official proof that they were plague free. Kinyoun refused to back down "unless ordered by Secretary of Treasury or Surgeon-General."

On June 16, lawyers for Wong Wai, the merchant who brought the first court case in May, went to Judge Morrow again. Wong had business in Eureka, California, a coastal city north of San Francisco, and he had tried to buy a steamship ticket there. His lawyers charged that Kinyoun would not let Wong board the ship without proof that he'd received the Haffkine vaccine. Kinyoun, they said, was ignoring the judge's May 28 ruling that allowed travel by Asians to other parts of California.

Judge Morrow ordered Kinyoun to appear in court to answer the charges. Kinyoun worried that the judge might send him to jail for contempt of court, even though he was carrying out instructions by his superiors in Washington.

At the hearing, Kinyoun testified that his concern was only with travel from San Francisco to other states. He told steamship companies they could sell tickets for in-state travel without health certificates. He denied ever meeting Wong Wai or stopping him from buying a ticket to Eureka.

The legal proceedings didn't go well for Kinyoun. The court refused to consider evidence he provided. The government attorney, who was supposed to provide his defense, was incompetent. Kinyoun felt abandoned by Wyman, who wasn't doing enough to help. Everyone involved seemed to be against him.

The stress of the past months had taken its toll on his health, and he suffered from severe stomach pains. These legal troubles made things worse.

A HATED MAN

Kinyoun had powerful enemies: Governor Gage and his political allies, the press, businesses, and much of the public.

Gage wanted Kinyoun's head. The governor complained that plague rumors, ill-advised quarantines, and travel restrictions hurt California's business and trade. Gage suggested that the bacteria, which Kinyoun claimed came from the victims' bodies, were really plague cultures imported from other countries. A newspaper commenting on the governor's accusations said, "Perhaps some inadvertently got loose in Kinyoun's bubonic pig pen."

The San Francisco newspapers called for "the removal from office of this incompetent and mischievous official." They referred to the cordon as the Kinyoun quarantine. "The harm which a pig-headed mischief-maker can do when intrusted with official power is now clear to us and we must get rid of Kinyounism by getting rid of Kinyoun."

Kinyoun heard that someone placed a $7,000 bounty on his life, and he started carrying a gun for protection.

Members of the Republican Party warned President McKinley that the plague controversy could hurt his chances in California during the November presidential election. The president and Wyman wanted to avoid a fight that could have serious political repercussions. They decided to ease the tensions in California.

On June 18, Wyman sent a telegram to Kinyoun: "Withdraw

In a cartoon from the *San Francisco Call*, June 19, 1900, Kinyoun sweats as he appears with his lawyer before Judge Morrow. His test animals gather at his feet. The *Call* used the rat, guinea pig, and monkey to remind readers that plague in the city was a fake.

all inspections until further orders." The federal restrictions against travel from San Francisco would end.

Kinyoun was afraid this wouldn't be enough to satisfy Judge Morrow and save him from jail.

On the morning of July 3, he stood before the judge, anxiously waiting to hear the verdict.

Morrow read his decision: "Kinyoun did not violate the order of the court in restraining [Wong Wai] . . . from departing from the city and county of San Francisco for the port of Eureka."

Kinyoun could hardly believe it. He was off the hook.

But the people of San Francisco didn't care what the judge said. They hated Joseph Kinyoun. There was no plague, and he had overreacted. Thanks to him, the rest of the country had shunned San Francisco over nothing. They wanted Kinyoun, the mayor, and the Board of Health gone.

Kinyoun realized that he had become the scapegoat in the fight over plague's existence in San Francisco. He knew he had failed at playing politics. His opponents criticized and blocked everything he did to control the threat of plague. He wrote his uncle, "I am at war with everybody out here."

———◆———

On July 5, two days after the judge cleared Kinyoun of contempt, Lee Wing Tong died in the city hospital. His doctor said he suffered from typhoid fever.

The diagnosis was wrong. An autopsy revealed that the man had a large groin bubo and swollen lymph glands under his arm. Lab tests proved that his body contained plague bacteria.

The dying wasn't over.

CHAPTER TEN

NO END IN SIGHT

> "Eradicate this pest hole from San Francisco before it menaces still further the whole country."
>
> —Joseph Kinyoun, 1900

On November 1, 1900, the bodies of Yung Moon Li Chee and her nine-year-old daughter, Yung Wah Noui, were found at 802 Dupont Street in Chinatown. A large, ugly bubo bulged from the mother's left thigh.

Kinyoun watched as the health department surgeon performed an autopsy on the little girl's body. Afterward, he checked the tissue for microbes.

The test results left no doubt. Her lungs were infected with plague bacteria. The child had died of pneumonic and septicemic plague.

The mother and daughter weren't the first suspicious deaths at that apartment. A week earlier, a twenty-three-year-old woman had died there, too. At the time, her death was labeled as sudden kidney failure.

In mid-September, the police surgeon had removed the body of a Chinese schoolteacher from the same apartment. Based on the deceased man's health history, the doctor labeled the case as death from pneumonia. After seeing these two new plague cases, he began to think it had actually been pneumonic plague.

Kinyoun suspected that all four victims had plague.

While the governor, press, and Chinese insisted that the disease did not exist, the outbreak kept growing.

STILL FILTHY

By the end of 1900, Kinyoun had used bacteriology to confirm 22 plague victims in San Francisco. Most were Chinese males. Four were Chinese females. The one white male victim, age thirty, died in the hospital after five days and was believed to have regularly visited Chinatown's opium dens. The lone white woman was a nurse at the city's Children's Hospital. No one knew how or where she had been infected.

Kinyoun was certain there had been at least twice as many deaths. Some of the suspicious corpses were too decomposed to test. Health authorities surely missed bodies in the Chinatown maze. They had been searching for cases only in one area of San Francisco. Wasn't it possible that plague deaths had occurred elsewhere in the city and been overlooked?

Surprisingly, every plague victim had died. Kinyoun never heard of a plague outbreak with 100 percent fatalities. This proved, he informed Wyman, "that the mild cases of plague have not been recognized as plague, but have been treated as other diseases." Maybe if they had found some of the victims earlier, they could have saved them with the Yersin serum.

Kinyoun was disheartened that the recent deaths showed how the plague-affected area within Chinatown had expanded. Politics, not science and medicine, were deciding the fate of the neighborhood.

Since summer, the health department inspections and disinfection in Chinatown had nearly stopped because neither the city nor state governments would supply the money and manpower. "The sanitary condition of Chinatown is no better," Kinyoun wrote Wyman. The streets were once again filled with rubbish, and people were living in unsanitary basement rooms.

He hoped people in San Francisco and California woke up from their dream and realized how serious the plague threat was. In his opinion, "plague will exist in Chinatown, San Francisco, until the district now occupied by the Chinese has been depopulated and destroyed."

HANG KINYOUN!

On January 8, 1901, Governor Gage presented his annual message to the California legislature. In it, he accused Kinyoun and San Francisco officials of falsely claiming that an epidemic of plague had struck the city.

The governor asked the legislature to pass a law making the importation of plague cultures "a felony punishable by life imprisonment." Gage also wanted to make illegal the laboratory culturing of plague bacteria, unless the state authorities allowed it.

The same day, a California state senator proposed a resolution demanding that President McKinley remove "Dr. J. J. Kinyoun from further service as quarantine officer."

In the legislature's debate that followed, one senator charged that Kinyoun maliciously tried "to slander the fair name of the State" by saying there was plague. Kinyoun was a "man of black and malignant heart" and "deserved to be hanged for quarantining the State."

Kinyoun was outraged by the insinuation—no, the allegation!—that he had faked the plague outbreak. "I [am] being disgraced

ABOVE: **Governor of California Henry T. Gage (1852–1924), in 1901.**

BELOW: **Gage and members of the state legislature wanted Kinyoun fired and his plague testing stopped.**

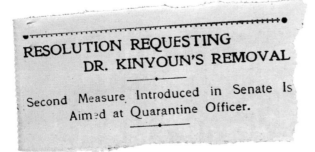

RESOLUTION REQUESTING
DR. KINYOUN'S REMOVAL

Second Measure Introduced in Senate Is Aimed at Quarantine Officer.

and discredited," he wired Wyman the same day. "Situation demands action be taken by you or allow me to defend myself."

BRING IN THE EXPERTS

Surgeon General Wyman couldn't let California and its governor continue claiming there was no plague. The state was threatening to interfere with federal inspections of incoming ships and testing for contagious diseases at the ports. Wyman had to stop this.

In mid-January 1901, he arranged for the secretary of the treasury, who oversaw the Marine-Hospital Service, to appoint a federal commission of three nationally respected scientists. These men worked with plague bacteria in the laboratory. They had firsthand experience with victims in Hong Kong, India, and the Philippines. Their task: find out whether or not plague exists in San Francisco.

Wyman picked three scientists without ties to the federal government. He hoped critics would be satisfied that the commission was neutral in the plague debate. With luck, its independent report would put to rest, once and for all, the controversy in California.

On Sunday, January 27, the three scientists— all in their thirties—gathered in a San Francisco hotel after traveling across the country by train. Simon Flexner was a pathologist from the University of Pennsylvania. Lewellys Barker was professor of anatomy at the University of Chicago. Frederick Novy, from the University of Michigan, had doctorate degrees in chemistry and medicine and studied bacteriology with Koch and Pasteur.

The men knew what they were up against. Even before they started, the press called them "youthful and inexperienced." Novy

The 1901 San Francisco plague commission (left to right): Lewellys Barker (1867–1943), Simon Flexner (1863–1946), Frederick Novy (1864–1957)

wrote his wife: "The newspapers and gov[ernor] feel that they must not be guided by bacteriological evidence. They will in the end lambaste us just as they have done to Kinyoun should we find plague."

IS IT PLAGUE?

For two weeks, the scientists studied conditions in Chinatown. Kinyoun and other members of the Marine-Hospital Service kept their distance to show that the commission was independent of the federal government.

KINYOUN AT SACRAMENTO UNDER ASSUMED NAME

Secret Commission to Investigate Alleged Existence of Bubonic Plague in California.

Despite this sensational headline from February 1, 1901, the commission was not secret and Kinyoun was not using an assumed name.

San Francisco officials cooperated, hoping this would finally resolve the plague problem. Then maybe the city's business and trade could return to normal.

The Six Companies provided an interpreter to help the commissioners. Chinese leaders realized they couldn't stop the federal investigation, but their representative might ease the impact on Chinatown's residents. The leaders ordered people to report all illnesses to the Six Companies offices.

Commission members and the Chinese representative checked the sick and examined the deceased. The majority of illnesses turned out to be chronic ones such as tuberculosis and heart disease.

They investigated 13 deaths. The scientists tried to respect the Chinese community's objection to autopsies. In most cases, they made only small cuts on the bodies to obtain samples of lymph glands and spleens for bacteriological testing. They found that 6 of the 13 had died of bubonic plague.

One was a twelve-year-old girl who had been checked by a commissioner when she first became sick. At that time, she showed no obvious symptoms of plague, and he thought her slight temperature was a sign of mild typhoid fever. But after she died suddenly five days later, tests revealed plague bacteria in her spleen.

When the commissioners completed their work, they wrote in their official report, "[We] conclude beyond possible doubt that cases of bubonic plague were occurring among the Chinese."

Lewellys Barker later told a group of physicians: "Every pathologist in San Francisco, except possibly one, agreed that this disease was plague, while those who opposed that view were men without sufficient training to recognize it."

UNFAIR!

Governor Gage was furious with the report. He protested to President McKinley, saying it was unfair. This plague nonsense had been concocted by an overzealous health department and one Joe Kinyoun.

The governor tried to keep the results quiet by convincing San Francisco newspapers not to report on them. Tourism and trade had already been hurt by Kinyoun's lies.

When Kinyoun heard what Gage was up to, he wasn't surprised. He had spent enough time battling the governor to know that he "will not try to discover the truth if he can escape doing so."

In April 1901, Wyman officially released the plague commission's full report to the press and to health authorities across the country. Governor Gage found himself forced into a corner. Other states had put quarantines on California, and they wouldn't lift them until they were assured that Chinatown was cleaned up and the threat of plague over. President McKinley warned that he would have to close the U.S. Army's headquarters in San Francisco if California didn't take steps to control the outbreak.

Faced with these threats, Gage reluctantly put state support and funds behind San Francisco's anti-plague efforts. Yet he refused to admit that there had ever been a single case there.

President William McKinley (1843–1901) on September 5, 1901, as he gave his final speech. The next day, he was fatally shot in Buffalo, New York.

He agreed to allow the Marine-Hospital Service to manage the operation . . . but only if Joe Kinyoun left California.

FAREWELL AND GOOD RIDDANCE

The governor got his way. In early April 1901, Surgeon General Wyman sent Kinyoun a message. He was to leave Angel Island and report to a post in Detroit, Michigan.

This was a demotion, and Kinyoun knew it.

He had seen the danger of plague. He had taken the necessary steps to prevent its spread within San Francisco and to the rest of the nation. He had done what Wyman directed. The commission vindicated him.

Despite that, self-interested politicians and an irresponsible press vilified him, called him a liar and cheat, and ruined his reputation.

It was some comfort to Kinyoun that a few people came to his defense. John Williamson, the president of the San Francisco Board of Health, wrote that Kinyoun had been "brutally maligned and scandalously misrepresented by persons desirous of making political capital."

Several California legislators wrote in a report that Kinyoun "had fearlessly held to the truth." One California medical journal called the governor's words and actions against Kinyoun "the most disgraceful, most pitiable, and humiliating chapter in the medico-political history of California."

But Kinyoun was bitter that Walter Wyman and the federal government hadn't done enough to support him.

Disillusioned with the Marine-Hospital Service, to which he'd given so much of his life, Kinyoun quit a year later, in 1902. He took his bacteriology expertise to private industry and other public health organizations.

Fighting plague in San Francisco remained one of the most frustrating experiences of his life.

Kinyoun's transfer was full-page news. He was actually sent to Detroit, Michigan, not St. Paul.

The San Francisco Call.

SAN FRANCISCO, TUESDAY, APRIL 16, 1901.

DR. KINYOUN RECEIVES ORDERS TRANSFERRING HIM AND ALL HIS PLAGUE THEORIES TO ST. PAUL

Surgeon General of the Marine Hospital Corps Heeds Protests of San Francisco Commercial Bodies---Dr. Carmichael of Honolulu Succeeds Him as Quarantine Officer

CHAPTER ELEVEN

CHANGES AT THE TOP

"Rats Must Go"
—Los Angeles Times, 1903

Most of San Francisco's rats were Norway rats (also called sewer or brown rats), the most common rat species in the United States.

N ow that Governor Gage was cooperating, or at least not interfering, the Marine-Hospital Service started its own vigorous attack on the Chinatown outbreak.

To manage the new anti-plague campaign, Wyman assigned Joseph White, one of his senior officers. White worked with seven other medical officers as well as local doctors and state and city employees. Instead of using Angel Island, as Kinyoun had, the Service set up a special plague laboratory and morgue on Merchant Street, half a block from the edge of Chinatown.

Every day, Service medical officers made inspections of Chinatown, accompanied by a Chinese interpreter, checking for plague cases among the sick. Did the person have a fever? Swollen glands? Tender spleen?

When the health department alerted them to suspicious

deaths, the officers performed autopsies and tested tissue samples for plague bacteria.

If officers found a victim, workers disinfected the buildings where the person lived and died. The sick were taken to a hospital and isolated. Nobody close to a patient was quarantined except in pneumonic cases. Anyone who had been exposed was monitored and given Yersin serum, if he or she agreed to it.

By the end of June 1901, nearly every house in Chinatown had been disinfected and fumigated at least once since the first plague case in March 1900.

The Chinese were glad to see a change from the disruptive quarantines and isolations that hurt businesses and families. But they still distrusted the intrusive medical and sanitary inspectors prowling around their neighborhood.

Despite the spring cleanup, people continued to get plague. By December 1901, more than four dozen had been confirmed as victims of the outbreak. Most were Chinese men. A few were Japanese or white. Only 3 survived.

The death toll was much lower than in Asia, a relief to the Service. Quarantines. Disinfection. Fumigation. Inoculation. Inspection of incoming ships. Wyman thought it all helped, yet none of it stopped San Francisco's epidemic.

GAGE GONE

Governor Gage's attitude about plague hadn't changed since March 1900 and the first quarantine. To him, the low death toll meant that these supposed victims didn't have the disease. If they did, there would have been thousands of dead, just as there were all over the world.

During the fall of 1901, the governor ended his support of Chinatown's cleanup. Without state money, the San Francisco anti-plague campaign slowed down.

Unfortunately, the outbreak didn't. In late summer and through the fall of 1902, the number of cases spiked, with about 30 new Chinatown victims, every one a fatality.

The news wasn't all bad, though. Amid charges of corruption and disapproval of the way Gage handled the plague crisis, the Republican Party chose not to nominate him for another term. In November, the voters elected a new governor, Republican George Pardee, a physician.

Until his last day in office in January 1903, Gage denied that plague ever existed in the state. In his farewell message to the California legislature, he again attacked Kinyoun, whose "ignorance and vicious conduct" led to "inaccurate reports growing out of reckless investigations."

The officers of the Public Health and Marine-Hospital Service (its new name as of 1902) were glad to see Gage go. They weren't alone.

George Pardee (1857–1941), elected governor of California on November 4, 1902

The Los Angeles Board of Health blamed him for interfering with the Service's efforts and endangering the entire state. "If the whole thing had been turned over to the Marine Hospital Service in the beginning," said one doctor on the Board, "there would have been little harm done. This thing of trying to deny or keep quiet such a condition of affairs has caused all the trouble."

George Pardee, the new governor, agreed that San Francisco had a plague outbreak. With everyone working together to end it, he declared, the state could convince the rest of the country that California was a safe place to visit and do business.

Factions that once opposed the Service joined the anti-plague effort. They recognized that the state faced a quarantine by the rest of the nation unless it made a serious effort to control plague. California's Board of Health, the San Francisco government, Chinese organizations, and business groups vowed their support.

They pledged to do what was necessary to ensure "that all danger from the bubonic plague may be eradicated."

Chinatown underwent a new, intense cleanup. From February to June 1903, workers demolished ramshackle buildings and hauled away garbage. They disinfected the neighborhood's buildings with 14 tons of bleaching powder, 600 pounds of mercury bichloride, and 1,600 gallons of carbolic acid. Once again, Chinatown's air reeked of chemicals.

BLUE IN TOWN

In May 1903, Surgeon General Wyman assigned Rupert Blue to lead the continuing anti-plague campaign.

Blue had the right qualities to pull everyone together. Born in North Carolina in 1867, he grew up on a plantation in South Carolina and possessed the southern friendliness and charm that helped smooth ruffled feathers. His tall, muscular stature and his hobby as an amateur boxer gained him the respect of the tough western men with whom he negotiated.

Blue joined the Marine-Hospital Service in 1892 at the age of twenty-five after attending medical school at the University of Maryland. During the years before Wyman assigned him to San Francisco, Blue served in cities throughout the United States and in Italy. He treated patients in marine hospitals, inspected ships, and screened immigrants.

Like Wyman, Blue devoted himself to his work. His seven-year marriage hadn't withstood the strain of his long absences and frequent reassignments, and he and his wife divorced in 1902.

Rupert Blue (1867–1948), around the time of San Francisco's plague outbreak

Blue had been stationed in San Francisco before, first at the Angel Island quarantine station. Then later, off and on since 1901, he had returned to the city to assist with the Service's anti-plague campaign. He was familiar with Chinatown and the complicated, contentious politics of San Francisco and California.

Using more tact than Kinyoun had, Blue maneuvered around the politicians to guarantee that the city and state continued to financially support the plague efforts. The sanitation work was helping. But people continued to die of plague—7 more that summer. Fewer cases showed up in 1903 than during the previous three years, and Blue wanted to keep it that way.

He recognized that rats spread plague, although he didn't understand how. The role of the flea remained a mystery—at least to Blue and the rest of the Service. Still, he knew he should target the rodents.

When Kinyoun pushed for destroying rats in 1900, the health department didn't have enough money to do a thorough job. The recent disinfection and fumigation seemed to have lowered the rat population. But Blue believed a dangerous number of infected rodents were scampering around Chinatown.

A dead rat tagged and ready for examination by the U.S. Public Health and Marine-Hospital Service in San Francisco

He ramped up the rat-killing. The city's chemist concocted a poison bait to use in the sewers. San Francisco put a bounty on rats turned in to the Merchant Street headquarters. Soon the laboratory was filled with rats. Between June 1903 and June 1904, the Service examined two thousand live rats and one thousand dead ones. Of those, twenty-two were infected with plague bacteria.

To some people, that seemed like a small number. Blue realized they had caught only a small percentage of the rodents. Even a single infected rat could cause multiple human deaths.

But killing and trapping wasn't enough because other rats moved into cleared-out areas. The only way to keep plague-infected

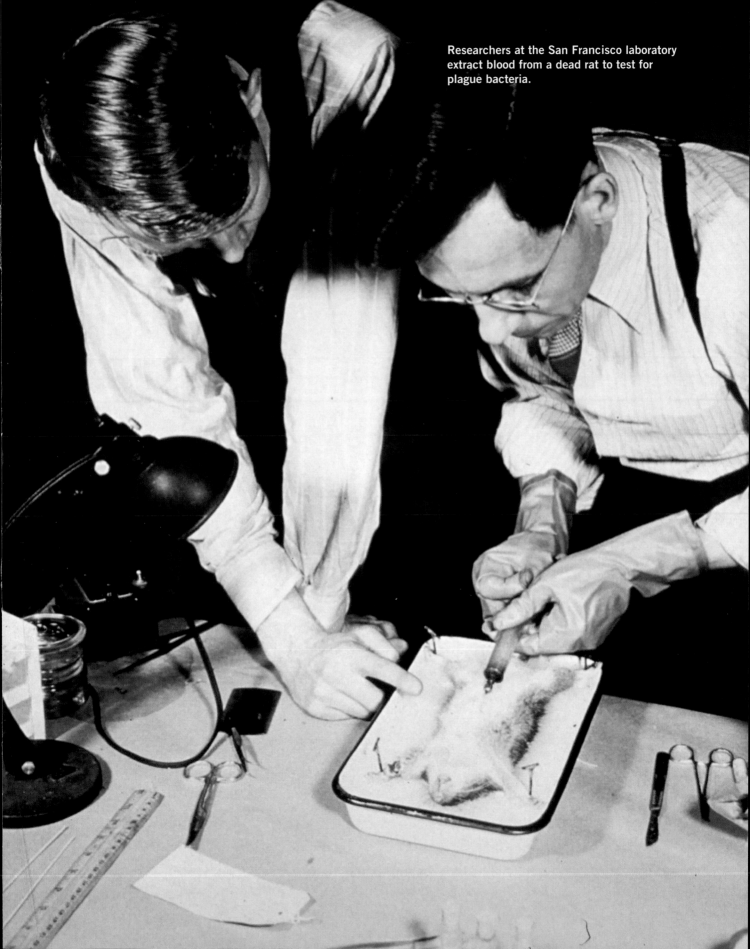

Researchers at the San Francisco laboratory extract blood from a dead rat to test for plague bacteria.

Workers prepare to burn debris in a San Francisco backyard where they found rat nests under flooring boards.

rats away from people was to rat-proof homes and businesses in Chinatown.

Inspectors searched for places where rats could enter buildings. City workers plugged cracks and holes in basement walls with brick and cement. They pulled up the wooden flooring, under which rats nested, and poured cement floors so that rodents couldn't burrow into basements.

Gradually, the number of human plague cases dropped. The outbreak finally seemed to be slowing down.

FINAL VICTIM

Matilda Soto lived close to the town of Concord in Contra Costa County, a farming area about 30 miles (48 kilometers) northeast of San Francisco. The daughter of Irish immigrants, she married Frank Soto in 1891. By 1904, she and Frank had eight children.

On the morning of February 24, 1904, the thirty-nine-year-old woman felt dizzy and nauseated. She was nearly seven months pregnant, so at first she didn't think much about it. That afternoon, she noticed a tender swelling under her left arm. By the next day, she was running a fever of 105 degrees Fahrenheit (41 degrees Celsius). She had a headache and was vomiting.

A doctor came. When he saw the swelling, he knew what it was. Bubonic plague. He immediately called the Service's plague headquarters in San Francisco.

B. J. Lloyd, a Service medical officer, traveled to the house on February 29. Soto's baby had already been born prematurely and died. About fifteen minutes after Lloyd arrived, the woman died, too.

Before the undertaker took away Matilda's body, Lloyd asked the family's permission to examine it for plague. Her relatives would not allow a complete autopsy, so instead, he carefully removed the swollen lymph nodes from under her arm.

A Service medical officer examines tissue samples for *Yersinia pestis* at the San Francisco plague laboratory.

Working in the local doctor's office, Lloyd prepared a slide from the material and viewed it under the microscope. No doubt about it. He was looking at plague bacteria. Lloyd warned the undertaker to wear rubber gloves when he embalmed the woman's body and to burn anything it soiled.

Back at the San Francisco laboratory, Lloyd cultured the material from Soto's nodes and injected it into test animals. They all died. The tests confirmed that Matilda Soto was a plague victim.

Her husband claimed she hadn't left the house for many weeks. No one else in the family was sick. How could she have caught plague from anyone?

Rupert Blue wondered if the woman had been infected by food or clothing that came into the home from somewhere else. Blue didn't know it yet, but a very different source was to blame.

Matilda Soto was the final victim of the San Francisco plague outbreak. She was the first to die outside the city. She would not be the last.

THE DEADLY TALLY

After four years, the epidemic had run its course. The number of victims varies, depending on the source. One reliable count identifies 121 victims in the city, of whom 118 died. In an additional 5 cases, the victims likely had been infected in a nearby community outside the city limits. Four of them died.

Most of the cases were bubonic with 97 percent dying, a rate far higher than bubonic plague's usual 40 to 60 percent. The doctors at the Merchant Street laboratory believed this was because the Chinese had not reported milder cases of plague. Usually, the Service saw only the dead.

Most victims were men—the majority of Chinatown residents. Seven were children. Almost all were Chinese. For some in the medical profession, the lopsided numbers confirmed that Asians were more susceptible to plague than other races. Not until several years later would they learn the truth: San Francisco's Chinese population had been unlucky enough to live near the harbor where plague entered the city. Infected rats and their fleas had thrived in their neighborhood.

A single case connected to San Francisco's outbreak occurred outside California. Frederick Novy, one of the three scientists on the 1901 commission, took samples of plague bacteria back to his University of Michigan laboratory to study. In early April 1901, a young medical student in his lab, Charles Hare, somehow became infected while working with the microbe. He never knew, or admitted, how the bacteria entered his nose or mouth.

When Hare became ill, Novy recognized the symptoms: high fever, nausea, and bloody mucous. He tested Hare's sputum. The young man had pneumonic plague.

Hare isolated himself in a special two-room building and began injections of the Yersin serum. His regular roommate, a fellow student, feared he might have been infected, too, since pneumonic plague was so contagious. He volunteered to care for Hare. Neither man was expected to survive.

One month later, Hare had recovered enough to leave the building. The resulting damage to his heart, however, caused health problems until his death at age fifty. His roommate used disinfectants to keep himself from being contaminated during their confinement. He never became sick.

THE END?

In April 1905, a year after Matilda Soto's death, Wyman ordered the closing of the Service's plague laboratory in San Francisco. The federal and local public health teams finally succeeded in "eradicating plague in the Chinese district of San Francisco." Many in the Service believed it would have happened sooner if they hadn't been forced to battle plague-deniers like Governor Gage.

The city's board of health publicly thanked Blue for his part in improving the city's sanitation and, as a result, its business prosperity.

By 1905, plague had reached six continents, probably carried by infected ship rats. Many of these places had never before been

struck by plague. In South America, it spread to Brazil, Chile, Peru, and Argentina. Russia had the most cases in Europe, but a few also occurred in the port cities of Great Britain, Portugal, and Spain. Compared with the horrors of the Second Pandemic, Europe remained relatively unscathed.

In Africa, plague broke out in Egypt, South Africa, Madagascar, and East Africa. It struck the coastal areas of Australia. In Asia, the hardest hit continent, epidemics continued in China with additional cases in Japan, Siam (Thailand), Singapore, and the Middle East. In India, the disease struck 1.4 million people from July 1904 to June 1905, killing 1.2 million of them.

In the United States, public health officers congratulated themselves on stopping plague in San Francisco before it spread throughout the country, the way it had in China and India.

What they didn't realize was that the bacteria had already escaped.

CHAPTER TWELVE

EARTHQUAKE!

"Frisco Doomed"
—*Guthrie [OK] Daily Leader, April 18, 1906*

While most San Franciscans slept early Wednesday morning, April 18, 1906, the ground under them shifted. Twenty seconds later, at 5:12 a.m., the earth ruptured along a fault line stretching for about 300 miles (483 kilometers). The earthquake's epicenter was only a couple of miles away from the city.

For nearly a minute, the ground shook violently, tossing people from their beds. When it stopped, San Francisco was in ruins. Buildings crumbled. Tons of bricks, stone, and broken glass tumbled. Streets buckled.

Still wearing nightclothes, tens of thousands of terrified people scrambled out of their destroyed homes into the morning chill.

The disaster would soon get worse.

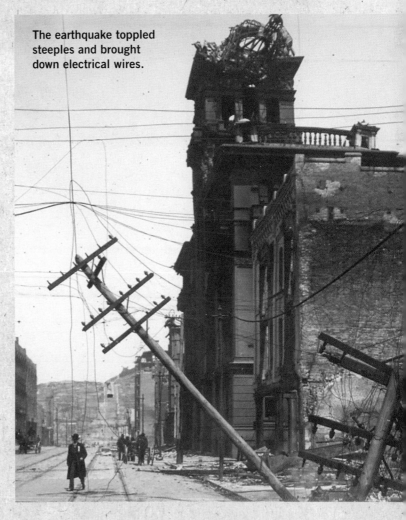

The earthquake toppled steeples and brought down electrical wires.

119

After the earth stopped moving, fire consumed the city.

Gainesville Daily Sun

VOL. XXIII, NO. 60   GAINESVILLE, FLORIDA, THURSDAY, APRIL 19, 1906   TEN CENTS A WEEK

TERRIBLE EARTHQUAKE IN SAN FRANCISCO

The Call=Chronicle=Examiner

SAN FRANCISCO, THURSDAY, APRIL 19, 1906.

EARTHQUAKE AND FIRE: SAN FRANCISCO IN RUINS

The sky to the east and south turned orange. Sparked by downed electrical wires and fueled by gas escaping from broken pipes, a massive fire tore through the city. Firefighters tried to douse the flames, but the inferno's heat drove them back. In a desperate attempt to slow the fire's advance, they used dynamite to blow up buildings in its path. The explosions created new fires.

During the next two days, headlines across the country broke the news of the disaster, one of the worst America had ever experienced. "Stricken San Francisco Doomed; Fire Beyond Control; Firemen in Despair"; "The City of San Francisco Is Doomed To Destruction by Fire Fiend."

The Paducah Sun.

VOL. XVIII. NO. 98. PADUCAH, KY., FRIDAY EVENING, APRIL 20, 1906. 10 CENTS PER WEEK.

SAN FRANCISCO A MASS OF RUINS

Unfortunate People of San Francisco Facing Starvation With Other Woes.

THE FIRE IS NOW UNDER CONTROL

Four Fifths of Once Beautiful City Is One Great Black Heap Today.

Horrors of This Situation May Overshadow The Work of Earthquake And Fire Prices Of Food Soar Skyward.

Flames Made Terrific Progress During Night, However

Story of The Great Fight With Unconq Elements Challenges The Ability The Pen To Tell.

Nothing Since The Burning of Rome By Nero Equals The Loss As It Will Finally Be.

Every Effort Is Being Made To Allay The Sufferir Homeless And Desolate Hosts.

THE GUTHRIE DAILY LEADER.

FRISCO DOOMED. Being Destroyed by Fire.

Frightful Cataclysm on the Pacific Coast--Two Earthquake Shocks Followed by Awful Conflagration.

Hundreds of Lives Lost and Millions of Dollars Worth of Property Destroyed.

The fire burned for three days, filling the air with smoke and soot. What the earthquake hadn't demolished, the raging fire gutted or leveled. More than 28,000 buildings were destroyed—from tall stone structures to wooden shacks. By the time it all ended, at least 225,000 of San Francisco's 400,000 people had lost their homes.

More than 3,000 people died—crushed in the ruins of collapsed buildings, struck by falling bricks and stones, or incinerated in the massive fire.

The nightmare wasn't over for the survivors.

Many managed to leave the city in cars or wagons or by ferries.

Flames ruined most of the city's business section.

But thousands of San Franciscans had no way to escape or nowhere to go. They converged on the city's parks and beaches, trying to get as far from the fire damage and teetering buildings as possible.

The Red Cross, U.S. Army, and local relief groups set up tent camps. Conditions were crude and unsanitary. The shaking ground had damaged sewers, spewing human waste and leaving parts of the city with no working toilets. The temporary latrines were soon overflowing, and people were forced to use uncovered holes in the ground.

San Franciscans wait for food in a bread line set up by relief groups.

With water mains cracked, unpolluted drinking water was hard to find. Garbage accumulated, piled near the camps or dumped on vacant lots where buildings once stood.

It wasn't long before diseases like typhoid fever, measles, diphtheria, and smallpox broke out among the people huddled together in the temporary camps.

And then, a year after the quake, the devastated city faced a new horror.

THE BUBO RETURNS

In May 1907, a critically ill tugboat sailor showed up at the U.S. Marine Hospital. Two days later, he was dead. The diagnosis: bubonic plague.

The sailor had been in port for six weeks. Doctors realized he must have caught the disease in the city. Had plague come to threaten San Francisco again?

Officers of the U.S. Public Health and Marine-Hospital Service waited with apprehension for more cases to surface. None did. Maybe the sailor had been an isolated case and there was nothing to worry about.

But in early August, a second sailor appeared at the Marine Hospital with a fatal case of plague. By the end of the month, the disease struck down 20 more people.

Service officers and the city health department nervously monitored reported illnesses and deaths. They began testing rats for plague. What they found confirmed their worst fears. Several people a day were collapsing with plague, and infected rats were dying all over the city. Was a terrible epidemic just beginning?

San Francisco's mayor sent an urgent telegram to President Theodore Roosevelt asking the Service to "assume immediate charge of the measures necessary to eradicate and prevent the spread of bubonic plague."

A man walks through part of Chinatown destroyed by the quake and fire.

The president passed the request to Surgeon General Wyman and urged him to "take action." Wyman didn't think twice about whom to assign as leader of his plague-fighting team. He sent Rupert Blue, the man Californians respected and praised for his work in 1903–05.

Blue arrived in San Francisco in mid-September 1907 ready to tackle his nemesis again. He found a city struggling in its slow recovery from the quake. Workers were tearing down damaged and dangerous structures, cleaning up rubble, and rebuilding homes and businesses. Thousands of people still lived in tents or makeshift shacks cobbled together from scavenged lumber and sheet metal.

These were conditions where plague thrived. His job wasn't going to be easy.

IT'S ALL ABOUT FLEAS

Blue knew more about his enemy than he had four years before.

In 1906, the Commission for Plague Investigations in India announced that experiments by other scientists confirmed what Masanori Ogata and Paul-Louis Simond discovered in 1897 and 1898: fleas carried plague bacteria from rat to rat and from rat to human. For nearly ten years, the scientific and medical communities ridiculed or ignored this important fact. The delay cost millions of people their lives.

Blue planned to use this knowledge to improve his anti-plague tactics. Since the disease wasn't contagious between people, except in the rare pneumonic form, there was no need for mass quarantines or disinfection of everything a victim touched. Flushing carbolic acid down sewers didn't destroy plague bacteria inside a rat or a flea's body, and it likely chased the rats elsewhere.

Burning down houses of plague victims probably killed some fleas and their bacteria. But fleeing rats escaped to other buildings and neighborhoods. Such harsh action only created public anger and resentment.

A couple left homeless by the quake prepares a meal in one of the city's tent camps.

Blue knew now that the only way unsanitary conditions led to plague was by giving rats easy access to food and places to hide. Wherever the rats went, so did their infected fleas. San Francisco had become a rat heaven. The streets in some areas were still filled with rubble. Thousands of people were cooking outside and leaving around food scraps as easy pickings.

Rupert Blue and his Service officers had their work cut out for them.

THE ANTI-PLAGUE CAMPAIGN

Within days of his arrival, Blue launched the new attack on plague. The city pledged funds, sanitary inspectors, and workers to assist the Service. By the end of September 1907, a team of hundreds of people was in full operation from Service headquarters in a two-story Victorian house on Fillmore Street.

When local doctors diagnosed a person with plague, an ambulance moved the patient to a special plague compound. The sick were isolated there in case the bacteria infected the lungs and produced the contagious pneumonic form. Doctors injected Yersin serum, trying to save those they could. About half the patients died.

When the earthquake struck, the shifting ground bent cable-car rails and tore up streets and sidewalks.

Workers immediately evacuated the patient's home and fumigated to kill infected rats and fleas. Inspectors searched the house and neighborhood for rats and their nests, laying traps and poison.

In one house, a man and woman, their three children, and a grandmother all developed plague. Only an eighteen-month-old boy was spared. Inspectors checked the house, and it seemed clean and tidy. When they tore up the wooden flooring in the house and backyard, they found nineteen dead rats, all infected with plague bacteria. After the rats died, their plague-carrying fleas had attacked the family.

Blue made sure that inspectors and workers received the Yersin serum or Haffkine vaccine as protection against the infected fleas they might encounter. As an added defense, inspectors released guinea pigs into buildings before they entered. Rat fleas swarmed to the fluffy rodents, a more desirable host than humans.

No one exposed to a plague victim was quarantined. If the victim had pneumonic plague, however, doctors gave Yersin serum to those who had been in close contact, just in case. They monitored anyone who lived or worked in a building where infected rats were found. After eight days without plague symptoms, the person was considered to be in the clear.

Blue did not recommend a mass immunization with the Haffkine vaccine. He believed it was probably only effective for six months and sometimes caused a painful reaction. During the first epidemic, he saw that most people refused it anyway. The outbreak hadn't exploded enough to make the vaccine necessary. Blue desperately hoped it never would.

The cleanup and rebuilding went on for years.

CHAPTER THIRTEEN

BLUE'S BRIGADE

> "Out of the houses the rats came tumbling."
> —San Francisco Call, *January 5, 1908*

By mid-November 1907, 135 people had come down with plague in the city still recovering from the devastating quake and fire.

One family was hit hard after two little boys buried a dead rat they'd found in an abandoned basement. Fleas leaped from the carcass onto their legs, and the boys unwittingly brought the infected insects home.

Within a week, one of the boys, his two-year-old sister, mother, father, and grandmother were sick with bubonic plague. The father died first, before a doctor had a chance to diagnose his illness and send him to the plague hospital. The other family members were treated in the hospital, but the twenty-seven-year-old mother developed pneumonic plague and died about two weeks after falling ill. The second little boy stayed healthy.

This San Francisco plague victim survived, but his leg had to be amputated.

Rat-catchers tag dead rats to show when and where the rodents were collected. One man (center) dips a rat trap into a bucket of disinfectant to kill the rat and its fleas.

Plague cases occurred all over the city, not in any single area as it had in 1900–04. The disease sickened people of all races, although most of the victims were white.

When plague spread through Chinatown in 1900, many San Franciscans believed the disease would never strike them. Now they were forced to change their thinking. "Plague was no longer a typically Oriental disease, nor wholly a filth disease, nor the peculiar affliction of vegetarians," wrote one city resident. "Yet it was curious how hard these ideas were to dispel, even in the face of the evidence furnished by white men's funerals."

"WHERE RATS GO PLAGUE WILL GO"

Blue had a simple strategy in his war on San Francisco's rats. Trap them. Poison them. Starve them. Destroy their hiding places.

Rat-catchers earned $2.50 a day plus 10¢ for every rat they found. To avoid fleabites, the men wore leather gloves, high-topped

shoes, and heavy pants with the leg bottoms tied with string. They placed live rats in cages covered with kerosene-soaked sacks so that the fleas couldn't escape. They tossed dead ones in metal cans with tight lids.

Poisoning squads concocted a special bait. They covered stale bread with a mixture of either arsenic or phosphorus paste combined with cheese, sugar, and bacon fat. By the end of the campaign, the squads had laid down nearly ten million poison croutons. Masses of dead rats floated in the bay, poisoned by bait placed in the sewers and around the wharves.

San Franciscans were warned to keep food away from rats by putting lids on garbage cans. Horse, cow, and chicken owners were told to keep grain feed in sealed containers.

A cartoon (above) and headline (below) from a March 1908 newspaper article about the plague campaign

City inspectors checked out buildings and advised owners how to rat-proof. If a property owner didn't make the required repairs, the city evacuated the building and condemned it. Most owners cooperated.

The rat-proofing guidelines:
- Reinforce foundations and basements with stone, brick, or cement.
- Raise wooden cottages and shacks 18 inches (46 centimeters) off the ground so that rat predators can keep the rodents away.
- Tear up wooden sidewalks under which rats hide, and replace them with concrete.
- Build concrete walls and floors in warehouses, markets, chicken yards, and stables where rats congregate for food. In one stable, trappers collected more than two hundred rats before it was rat-proofed.
- Fix openings in wood floors and around plumbing where rats can slip into a house. After one man died of plague, inspectors discovered holes in the floor beneath his bed. Under the wooden boards, they found a pile of rat corpses. As the rats died, their infected fleas had jumped on the sleeping man.

To prevent infected rats and their fleas from leaving or entering San Francisco's port, the Service's quarantine officers fumigated all outgoing and incoming boats and ships. They released the gas while the ships were in the bay, away from shore, so that the rats couldn't escape the poisonous fumes. After treating one ship before it set sail, officers discovered five hundred dead rats. The men repeated the process until they found no more corpses.

Workers in the Ratatorium dissect rats nailed to wooden shingles. The staff usually wore rubber gloves for protection.

THE RAT LAB

Blue ordered every rat caught alive or dead to be taken to the Service's Fillmore Street headquarters. Rat-trappers and homeowners turned in seven thousand to eleven thousand rats a week.

An annex to the main building became the rat lab and was nicknamed the Ratatorium. As the rats poured in, Service officers chloroformed the live ones and combed their fur to collect fleas. An entomologist identified each flea's species.

Blue hired rat-skinners to dissect the rats. Working at a lead-covered table, the men wore aprons and rubber gloves to reduce the chance of being infected by plague bacteria.

After dipping a dead rat in a chemical to kill remaining fleas, the rat-skinner nailed the body to a wooden shingle. Using a sharp blade, he carefully sliced open the rat's belly, revealing its internal organs. If he found an animal with signs of plague in the lymph glands, spleen, liver, or lungs, a pathologist and a bacteriologist examined and tested the body. When they finished, the corpses were burned.

The rat-skinners cut open as many as five hundred rats a day. It was messy, gory, and smelly work.

A local newspaper poked fun at Blue and his campaign against rats, calling him the Pied Piper of Hamelin:

"When Dr. Blue blew on his pipe:

    And ere three shrill notes the pipe uttered

    You heard as if an army muttered;

    And the muttering grew to a grumbling

    And the grumbling grew to a mighty rumbling;

    And out of the houses the rats came tumbling."

Blue's strategy started to work, and the number of human plague cases tapered off. But he knew it was too early to stop the war on rats.

Recent research from the Philippines showed that if 1 percent of trapped rats had plague, humans were in danger. When 2 percent were infected, the community faced a major epidemic. By December 1907, the Service found plague in 1.5 percent of San Francisco's trapped rats.

Blue was concerned. The flea population naturally dropped during the cold months. But when spring and summer returned, the increase in fleas might cause a fresh spike in human plague cases. Before warm weather arrived, they had to do more to control the rats, and he'd need the entire community to help.

SAN FRANCISCO UNITES

By late January 1908, with Blue's encouragement, all of San Francisco mobilized against plague. Nobody denied that the city had an outbreak. No one tried to hide the victims. No one blamed any particular group or race for causing it. People understood that plague was a threat to everybody.

Blue and other Service doctors spoke to churches, businesses, unions, and civic groups to explain the disease and the way people become infected.

In one speech, Blue urged two thousand employees of the Southern Pacific Railroad to do their part. "I intend to kill a rat or two myself tonight," he told the crowd, "and I want all of you to do the same. It is the noblest work you can do."

The Service was not above using scare tactics. Blue's top assistant warned audiences: "I want you to understand that if a quarantine is placed on San Francisco you people will imagine yourselves in the worst corner of hell." He went on, "The days following the disaster of April, 1906, will seem like a holiday picture compared to the days to be spent in a city quarantined for the bubonic plague."

CITIZENS' HEALTH COMMITTEE OF SAN FRANCISCO

TO ALL HOUSEHOLDERS

KILL THE RATS

TRAPS: The best trap for dwellings, stores, etc., is the large cage trap.

BAIT: To be changed daily between cheese, fish heads, chicken heads, fried bacon, fresh liver and pine nuts.

Bait to be tied on inner side of top of trap.

Smoke the trap after handling and before setting again for other rats.

Cover the trap except entrance with sacking.

Place trap near usual feeding place of rat.

Snap traps are best in butcher chops, bakeries and restaurants.

Bait should be tied on.

POISON: All druggists can furnish a good rat poison. Follow directions. Place in rat holes, beneath floors and in covered places. **DO NOT PLACE WHERE ACCESSIBLE TO CHILDREN.**

DISPOSITION OF RATS: On delivery of dead or trapped Rats at any Health Station, (see reverse side,) a bounty of 10c. per Rat will be paid. Rats should be carried to Station in closed tin boxes or cans.

IF NOT CONVENIENT TO TAKE RATS TO HEALTH STATION, TELEPHONE TO NEAREST STATION AND RATS WILL BE CALLED FOR AND BOUNTY PAID BY INSPECTOR ANSWERING CALL.

A Citizens' Health Committee flyer gives tips on how to kill rats.

The possibility of a national boycott of the city propelled businesses into cooperating and donating money for the anti-plague campaign. The Citizens' Health Committee raised nearly $200,000 to pay for more inspectors, extra workers to trap and poison rats, and men to fumigate buildings. The Committee passed out seven hundred thousand flyers to the city's residents with tips on trapping and poisoning rats.

The Women's Sanitation Committee spread the word to homemakers about how to keep rats out of their houses. The women inspected schools, restaurants, markets, hotels, and shops, checking for adequate rat prevention. When they saw a problem, they

GARBAGE

Clean up your own premises.

Keep all Garbage in Covered Metal Cans.

Keep covers closed.

This will starve the Rat.

Have garbage removed weekly or more frequently.

Don't allow garbage to be thrown on vacant lots around your premises.

Admit any authorized Health Inspector to your premises.

He is there for **YOUR** benefit.

Watch and Report for your own protection unsanitary conditions in your neighborhood.

Tell your neighbors to do the same.

A flyer with advice for reducing the rat population

reported it to the health department.

In the schools, teachers explained the danger of rats and fleas. Children did their part by collecting trash in their neighborhoods. Some turned in rats to the Service's Fillmore Street laboratory. The bounty of 10¢ a rat was welcome spending money.

NO MORE BUBONIC RATS

Plague attacked its last San Franciscan in February 1908. The young man eventually recovered. The 1900 outbreak had lasted four years. This time it was over in nine months.

Though counts vary, the most complete records show that from May 1907 to February 1908, plague infected 167 people in the city. The victims included more than two dozen children, the youngest only a month old.

Of the total, 78 died, a death rate much lower than the 97 percent of 1900–04. Prompt medical treatment saved many. More than 90 percent of the cases were bubonic. All the pneumonic and septicemic victims died.

Unlike the first outbreak, few victims were Asian, and Chinatown was not the center. In fact, nearly two dozen additional people developed plague outside of San Francisco, across the bay in neighboring communities.

In October 1908, the Service cut open its last infected rat. Trapping and poisoning continued, and the Service tested tens of thousands more rats through the winter months without finding any infected. At the beginning of March 1909, the Service and the city felt confident enough to announce the end of San Francisco's plague epidemic.

Between September 1907 and March 1909, the rat patrols estimated killing 2 million rats. At its laboratory, the Service processed more than 350,000 rats and collected 11,000 of their fleas. The officers tested 154,000 of the rats and found 398 infected with plague. That was a small percentage of San Francisco's rats, but it had been enough to cause an epidemic.

More than a thousand people were part of Blue's brigade— Service doctors and laboratory workers, building inspectors, fumigation and cleaning crews, rat-trappers, and poisoning squads. The care they took to avoid fleabites had been worth it. None of them became infected with plague.

A researcher checks a dead rat for signs of plague.

The Public Health and Marine-Hospital Service officers who fought San Francisco's 1907–09 plague outbreak. Rupert Blue is seated third from the left.

The plague campaign earned national headlines and admiration for the U.S. Public Health and Marine-Hospital Service, especially Rupert Blue. On March 31, 1909, the city and state celebrated "the success attending the work of plague eradication" with a banquet held at the Fairmont Hotel in Blue's honor. Four hundred people attended. On the menu was an ice-cream dessert shaped like a mousetrap with a rat's head sticking out.

Each member of Blue's team of Service officers received a medal. Blue was presented with a gold watch. "We needed a leader," California governor James Gillett said, "and we got Dr. Blue."

In his short speech to the crowd, Blue responded, "San Francisco has fought her battle and as one of you I am proud of the victory she has gained."

For his work overseeing the end of the outbreak, Blue later earned an award he coveted more than a watch. In January 1912, President William Howard Taft appointed him surgeon general after Walter Wyman died in a diabetic coma. Taft chose the forty-four-year-old Blue over several older and more experienced Service officers.

In its final report on the outbreak, San Francisco's Citizens' Health Committee ended with a warning: "The disease, to-day, is all over the world, and no one can tell where some migrating rat will carry it next."

Rupert Blue had a very strong hunch where plague would travel next. And it wasn't good news for the rest of America.

In 1908, the Citizens' Health Committee held an outdoor luncheon to celebrate the plague campaign's success. Rupert Blue was guest of honor. Several months later, the city and state celebrated again with an evening banquet at the Fairmont Hotel.

CHAPTER FOURTEEN

INTO THE WILD

"Once planted in this ideal soil, infection may never be uprooted or its growth and extension controlled."

—*Rupert Blue, 1910*

For Rupert Blue, the San Francisco outbreaks weren't over. He remained troubled by a few of the cases that occurred in the final months of the first epidemic.

In 1903, shortly before they died in the city, three of the plague victims spent time in Contra Costa County, across the San Francisco Bay. The outbreak's last victim, Matilda Soto, was infected and died in the same county in early 1904. No one could figure out how she had been infected. She had not left her home in months or been anywhere near San Francisco.

In mid-September 1903, the Service heard reports of thousands of wild ground squirrels dropping dead in an area of Contra Costa

Ground squirrel

County full of ranches and farms. Inspectors were never able to examine any of the dead animals to confirm plague. At the time, Blue failed to get the funding to mount an extensive search for infected ground squirrels. But he knew that rodents other than rats could die of plague. Why not ground squirrels? Had the human deaths been connected to infected squirrels?

Then, in June 1904, two boys from the county died a few days after hunting ground squirrels. The Service didn't have the chance to test or examine the victims' bodies for plague. Blue suspected "that the squirrels of Contra Costa County are already infected." Because these animals lived throughout California, it was, in his view, "a most serious matter indeed."

Plague struck the area again nearly two years later, in April 1906. A fourteen-year-old boy developed the disease in Oakland, a city on the same side of the bay as Costa Contra County. Two or three days before he fell ill, he had been hunting ground squirrels. Blue still didn't have proof, yet the evidence was mounting that these animals carried the plague bacteria.

DISTURBING CLUES

During the fall of 1907, as the post-earthquake outbreak intensified among San Francisco's residents, Blue learned that a handful of people also had plague in communities across the bay. When a Service officer investigated, he found plague-infected rats in Oakland.

The following summer, four months after the final victim fell ill in the city, the seven-year-old son of a rancher in Contra Costa County died of bubonic plague. Within the week, a man and woman in the same area died of it, too.

Trappers caught several sick ground squirrels, including one on the ranch where the boy lived. The animals were examined at the Service laboratory. All contained plague bacteria.

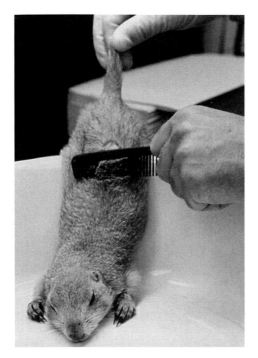

For the first time, Blue had the proof he was waiting for. The deadly microbe existed not only in rats and mice making their homes around humans but also in American rodents living in the wild.

The Service performed experiments to find out whether the ground squirrel's fleas would bite humans. They did.

Other tests revealed that San Francisco's city rats carried some of the same fleas typically found on wild ground squirrels.

The rats and ground squirrels had interacted, sharing their fleas. Now Y. *pestis* had a new rodent host.

No one knew how or when this happened. Infected city rats and their fleas could have hitched a ride with people and supplies going from San Francisco to surrounding rural areas. Possibly a ground squirrel came upon a rat nest where it picked up infected fleas. Or fleas jumped from a dead rat onto a passing ground squirrel.

To Blue, this discovery was momentous. "The demonstration of natural plague in the California ground-squirrel . . . ," he wrote, "is perhaps the most important observation of the anti-plague work of the Service in 1908."

During the next several years, the Service found hundreds of infected ground squirrels throughout the state. Between February 1908 and January 1916, at least 13 people fell ill with plague after their contact with these rodents.

The Service joined with the state to wipe out the ground squirrel population in California. Hired hunters shot and poisoned the animals. A new state law required farmers to kill ground squirrels on their property. Authorities set up a squirrel-free zone around the northern cities of San Francisco, Oakland, Alameda, and Berkeley to prevent reinfection of city rats.

Then, in August 1919, an Oakland man brought home several ground squirrels that he shot for food in a rural area near the city. Two days later, he had a bubo under his arm and congested lungs. Within the week, he was dead.

During his illness, the man had contact with 4 people who later developed pneumonic plague. They spread it to others. As soon as health authorities realized the sick people had plague, they isolated the patients in a hospital. That ended the outbreak. By then, 14 people had fallen ill, and 13 of them died.

The outbreak showed how difficult it was going to be to contain plague now that it infected America's rodents in the wild.

A hunter poses with the squirrels he shot in a rural area outside San Francisco, around 1909. Health authorities encouraged the killing of California's ground squirrels to stop the spread of plague.

INTO THE PORTS

While the Service was dealing with California's ground squirrel danger, Y. *pestis* kept up its relentless advance around the world.

When he became the new surgeon general in 1912, Rupert Blue acknowledged the international threat. Considering the way plague had spread by ships to every continent, he commented, "It would be surprising and quite accidental if ports of any size have escaped the infection."

To prevent another outbreak like San Francisco's, Service officers at all U.S. ports continued their thorough inspections of incoming ships. They required a metal disc, called a rat baffle, on mooring ropes. This stopped rats from scurrying along ropes from ship to shore, carrying infected fleas with them.

Officers monitored areas near the docks, trapping and dissecting rats and examining their fleas for Y. *pestis*. By detecting plague early, they had time to wage war on the rat population before infected fleas began biting humans.

Rats climbed ropes onto ships that transported them—and their plague-infected fleas—to ports throughout the world.

Despite these efforts, from 1907 to 1920, plague outbreaks occurred in ports along the West Coast and the Gulf of Mexico. Seattle, Washington. Los Angeles, California. New Orleans, Louisiana. Pensacola, Florida. Galveston and Beaumont, Texas. More than 100 people came down with plague. About half of them died.

In all these outbreaks, local and state health authorities, businesses, and the public cooperated with the federal government to fight the epidemic. The anti-plague campaigns were modeled on Blue's successful war against rats and fleas in San Francisco.

Y. *pestis* apparently never escaped from the Gulf Coast ports to take hold in the wild the way it did around San Francisco. This was partly because rat and human plague cases were controlled quickly and thoroughly. Another reason may be that fewer susceptible wild rodents lived in those areas because of the local temperatures, humidity, and habitats.

From the ports in Seattle and Los Angeles, plague might have spread from imported rats into populations of wild rodents such as the ground squirrel. There's not enough evidence to be sure.

Workers in New Orleans, around 1915, pose with traps, cages, and collection buckets they used to catch rats.

THE LOS ANGELES OUTBREAK

The Service faced its final human epidemic during the fall and early winter of 1924–25. For three and a half months, plague raced through a Los Angeles neighborhood of Mexican immigrants.

Starting as a bubonic infection, the outbreak turned into a deadly pneumonic nightmare when the bacteria traveled to the lungs of the second bubonic victim. Eventually, 32 people caught pneumonic plague. Only 2 survived. Of the 8 people with bubonic plague, just 3 lived. Authorities finally stopped the outbreak by isolating the contagious pneumonic victims before they infected other people.

Local, state, and federal governments launched a massive rodent-extermination program around Los Angeles. Crews trapped and poisoned hundreds of thousands of rats and ground squirrels in the city, the harbor, and the surrounding countryside. They found plague in both animals.

Investigators located infected rats near the victims' homes, and they suspected these rodents started the epidemic. It remained a mystery whether plague first entered Los Angeles through ship rats at the port, wild ground squirrels, or some other source.

OUT OF CALIFORNIA

The killing of ground squirrels in California went on for more than two decades as authorities tried to contain plague. In the end, the task proved to be impossible.

On May 21, 1934, a thirty-year-old Oregon sheepherder died after contact with an infected ground squirrel. During the next two years, scientists detected Y. *pestis* in the ground squirrels of Montana, Idaho, Nevada, and Utah.

Plague had escaped from California.

The bacterium found a permanent home in the blood of wild animals, especially burrowing rodents in the grasslands and semiarid areas of the United States. Today, it survives in seventeen western states from the Pacific Ocean into western parts of the Great Plains.

So far, scientists have discovered that Y. *pestis* naturally infects more than 200 species of mammals around the world, including about 75 species in the United States. Most are rodents. Only a few of these animals have a significant part in spreading plague. The bacterium does not infect birds, reptiles, or amphibians.

Some kinds of rodents carry the bacterium without the majority of their population falling sick. That allows Y. *pestis* to permanently survive in the wild because only a few individuals are likely to die of plague. Before they die, these susceptible animals may infect fleas, allowing the disease to spread. The more plague-resistant members of the group will survive and produce offspring, some of which will be susceptible and others resistant.

When the climate and food supply are more favorable, the populations of the mammal host and its fleas increase. The chances become greater that fleas infected with Y. *pestis* from the blood of their hosts will jump onto other mammals after the hosts die of plague.

Arrows show the ways plague is transmitted among populations of fleas, rodents, humans, and carnivorous mammals. Humans are considered dead-end hosts because plague bacteria rarely spread from one person to another.

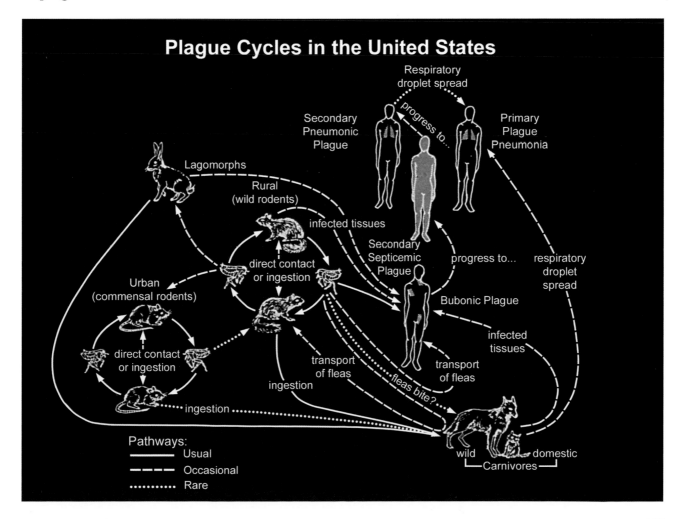

Plague Cycles in the United States

Respiratory droplet spread

Secondary Pneumonic Plague

progress to...

Primary Plague Pneumonia

Lagomorphs

Rural (wild rodents)

infected tissues

Urban (commensal rodents)

direct contact or ingestion

Secondary Septicemic Plague

progress to...

respiratory droplet spread

Bubonic Plague

direct contact or ingestion

transport of fleas

transport of fleas

infected tissues

ingestion

fleas bite?

ingestion

wild   domestic
Carnivores

Pathways:
——— Usual
- - - - - Occasional
·········· Rare

If infected fleas bite a mammal that is highly susceptible to plague, a deadly epidemic may break out in its population. Rodents that burrow or make nests are vulnerable because infected fleas can easily move among animals living in tight quarters.

In the United States, susceptible wild rodents include ground and rock squirrels, woodrats, and prairie dogs. Plague also strikes chipmunks, deer mice, voles, and rabbits.

If a person gets close to the fleas from an infected animal, he or she may be bitten and infected, too. That's more likely to happen when the animal lives around people, as the rat does.

This helps explain the human pandemics of the past fifteen hundred years. The original source of the plague bacterium might have been wild marmots or gerbils living in central Asia. Recent genetic studies indicate that Y. *pestis* evolved into a deadly microbe in that part of the world.

From there, it probably hitched a ride in fleas and rats transported by humans traveling the trade routes across continents and oceans. In countries around the globe, the bacterium found new hosts among local rodents and their fleas.

By the early 1900s, Y. *pestis* had arrived on the doorsteps of hundreds of San Franciscans . . . and in the burrows and nests of America's wild animals.

Plague is known to exist in wild animals in the countries in red. Humans may get plague if they have contact with infected animals or their fleas.

PLAGUE IN THE WILD

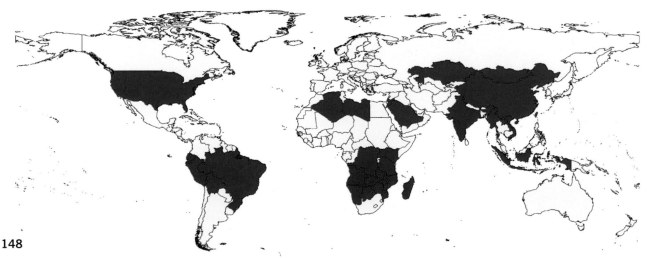

MAMMALS
IN THE **UNITED STATES** THAT **ARE SUSCEPTIBLE** TO **PLAGUE**

TOP LEFT: rabbit
TOP RIGHT: rock squirrel
BOTTOM: prairie dogs

A U.S. military poster from World War II informs soldiers how to avoid plague. The flea's head resembles the Japanese leader, Emperor Hirohito. In a similar poster, the flea looks like German leader Adolf Hitler.

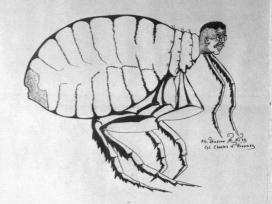

Know Your Enemy
THE FLEA

I CARRY PLAGUE

Don't Sleep In Rat Infested Houses
Don't Leave Food to Attract Rats and Mice

THE FLEA CONNECTION

Yersinia pestis depends mainly on fleas to spread. An adult flea gets its nourishment from a host's blood. Each flea species has its own preferred host mammal, but it may feed on others, too.

Of more than 2,500 known flea species, at least 125—and possibly as many as 250—have been found to carry the bacterium. Only a few dozen of them play key roles in spreading plague to other animals.

Biologists consider the Oriental rat flea, *Xenopsylla cheopis*, the most dangerous. It is more successful in transmitting plague bacteria than other kinds of fleas are. And, importantly, it infests the types of rats that live in close contact with humans.

When a rat is sick with plague, its blood contains millions of *Y. pestis*. A single meal for the *X. cheopis* could include a few thousand bacteria, enough to infect the flea. Sick rats can be infested with many fleas. This might be because the rats stop grooming themselves or because they have picked up fleas that jumped from dead plague-infected rats. That helps *Y. pestis* spread even faster and to more hosts.

If *X. cheopis* feeds on a dying rat and within about four days feeds on a healthy rat, the flea will likely pass *Y. pestis* to the second rat.

After these first days, the flea might temporarily lose its ability to transmit plague. But the bacteria continue to multiply inside its gut. Within about two or three weeks, they clog the upper part of the flea's digestive system, blocking future blood meals from passing farther down the gut and being digested. As a result, the flea feels hungry.

If the host dies from plague, the ravenous flea jumps onto a new one. It bites into the host's skin and sucks up a blood meal. But the blockage in the gut of the flea forces it to spew the fresh blood back into the bite wound. Some of the *Y. pestis* in the flea's body go along with the blood—hundreds, and perhaps thousands, of microbes. Fewer than ten can be enough to cause plague in the new host.

Xenopsylla cheopis, highly magnified, after it has fed. The host's red blood is visible inside the flea's digestive system.

In a digitally colored image from an electron microscope, plague bacteria (yellow) stick to the spines (purple) inside a *Xenopsylla cheopis* flea's digestive tract.

The flea, still starving, bites again and again. Each time, it may pass more bacteria into its mammal host, increasing the chances of the host falling ill with plague. Once *X. cheopis*'s gut is totally blocked, it dies of starvation after about five days.

In other kinds of fleas, *Y. pestis* never completely blocks the digestive system, or it doesn't create a clog at all. The fleas transmit the microbes in another way, perhaps on their contaminated mouth parts or in their saliva. Many of these fleas may pass along *Y. pestis* for a few days after becoming infected. In some cases, their gut also may become partially blocked, allowing them to survive several weeks, infecting more and more hosts with each bite.

Scientists continue to study the ways *Y. pestis*, fleas, and mammals interact. Why do the bites of some flea species transmit bacteria more readily than others? How long can *Y. pestis* survive inside a flea's body? How long can it live outside a mammal or flea host? The answers to these and other questions remain mysteries.

CHAPTER FIFTEEN

DISEASE UNDEFEATED

"Recent outbreaks have shown that plague may reoccur in areas that have long remained silent."

—World Health Organization, 1999

Sierra Jane, age seven, felt sorry for the dead squirrel she found by the family's picnic site at a Colorado campground. Without touching the animal, she tried to bury it. While she worked, she laid her sweatshirt on the ground.

Five days later, Sierra Jane awoke with a fever. Her leg hurt near her groin. She vomited, and her fever spiked to 107 degrees Fahrenheit (42 degrees Celsius). Soon she had seizures and became delirious.

Her alarmed father drove her to the closest emergency room. But Sierra Jane was so sick that doctors called for a medical helicopter to fly her 400 miles (644 kilometers) to a special hospital in Denver.

Doctors there found fleabites on Sierra Jane's body. Her parents mentioned the picnic.

"At that point I started putting all the pieces together,"

her doctor Jennifer Snow said later, "because I know animals carry the plague in that area."

Colorado hadn't had a human plague case for six years. Fortunately, Sierra Jane's doctors were alert to the possibility. "It's one of those things that you don't necessarily expect to see," said Wendi Drummond, another doctor who cared for the girl. "But it's definitely one of those things you don't want to miss."

Plague-infected fleas had jumped from the dead squirrel to Sierra Jane's sweatshirt and body.

If this had happened in 1912, Sierra Jane's chances of surviving bubonic plague would have been extremely low. The bacteria had already spread through her body, and she was gravely ill. Instead, it was 2012.

In the early 1940s, researchers discovered a drug that killed *Yersinia pestis*. Since then, they have developed additional effective antibiotics. As soon as the Denver doctors realized that Sierra Jane might have bubonic plague, they gave her these drugs. She spent almost three weeks in the hospital, but she didn't die. Antibiotics stopped the microbe's attack.

Yersinia pestis, stained and magnified

DEADLY *YERSINIA PESTIS*

The bacteria had stealthily entered Sierra Jane's body through a fleabite so tiny that she never noticed it.

Using tricks that scientists don't completely understand, Y. *pestis* outsmarts the body's defenses. Before Sierra Jane even felt sick, the bacteria had gained the upper hand.

The microbes can't move on their own. In a process that researchers continue to study, the bacteria are carried to a nearby lymph node, an immune-system battle station. Inside the node, the bacteria rapidly multiply. The node swells, producing a bubo.

Because most fleabites are on the leg, close to the ground,

buboes usually appear in the groin or thigh. If the bite is around the head, the swelling will be on the neck or behind the ears. When the infection enters on the hand or arm, the bubo will be in the armpit.

A less common pathway into the body is through a break in the victim's skin or through mucous membranes in the mouth, nose, or eyes. A person who handles the tissue or fluids from a plague-infected mammal can be infected through a cut on the hand.

Antibiotics save 95 percent of people at this stage in a bubonic infection.

INTO THE BLOOD

Sometimes, the bacteria leave the lymphatic system and enter the bloodstream. Carried throughout the body, billions of bacteria infect the organs. The exploding numbers completely overpower the immune system, organs fail, and the victim dies of secondary septicemic plague.

In about one-sixth of the plague cases in the United States during the past fifty years, the victim developed primary septicemic plague from the start. Bacteria from a fleabite or wound went directly into the bloodstream rather than into the lymph nodes.

With septicemic plague, Y. *pestis* disrupts the blood flow to small blood vessels under the skin or in organs, damaging the tissue. Death follows within days in nearly 100 percent of cases. Even with antibiotics, from a quarter to half of all septicemic patients die. Since no bubo forms, they are often not diagnosed with plague and treated in time.

In June 2015, just days before Taylor's sixteenth birthday, the Colorado high-school student felt feverish and achy, as if he had the flu. After he started coughing up blood four days later, he and his parents immediately headed for the hospital.

On the way, Taylor stopped breathing and died. Septicemic plague had taken his life before anyone realized why he was ill.

No one knows how he was infected. Public health investigators guessed he had been bitten by a plague-infected flea or handled an infected animal on or near his family's rural property.

Several U.S. plague cases have occurred in people who skinned infected rabbits, bobcats, or coyotes. An American biologist came down with plague after skinning an infected prairie dog in the laboratory. When she accidentally cut herself, the bacteria entered her body through the open wound. Antibiotics saved her life.

According to reports from other countries, people have developed a form of plague in their pharynx after swallowing raw meat from an infected animal. This results in swollen neck lymph nodes and fever.

INTO THE LUNGS

Pneumonic plague, the deadliest form, strikes in two ways. In secondary pneumonic plague, the bacteria enter the body through a fleabite or wound. They eventually are carried by blood into the lungs, causing infection there. When the victim sneezes or coughs, bacteria-laden droplets leave the lungs.

If another person breathes in the contaminated droplets, the *Y. pestis* bacteria will infect his or her lungs, causing primary pneumonic plague.

This is the only human plague that can be passed person-to-person, and it's not easy to get. Someone must be in close contact with a plague victim, within 6.5 feet (2 meters), and must breathe in the contaminated droplets. The last

Scientists in the Philippines, around 1912, wear protective masks while performing plague experiments. Only the pneumonic form of plague is contagious between humans.

confirmed cases of person-to-person plague in the United States occurred during the Los Angeles outbreak of 1924–25.

In 2014, however, a Colorado woman may have become the first victim of person-to-person transmission in ninety years. The outbreak began with a sick pit bull that infected its owner and two veterinary workers with pneumonic plague. Later, a fourth person—the woman—fell ill with pneumonic plague, too. Public health investigators weren't sure whether her infection came from the dog or its owner. The timing of her symptoms, however, pointed to the human owner, with whom she'd had close contact.

Antibiotics saved all four people, though the dog died. Eighty-eight other people who had close contact with the dog or the four patients were given antibiotics as a precaution. None became ill.

In the United States since 1950, only about half the pneumonic victims recovered.

DANGER IN THE SOUTHWEST

Since the night that plague killed Wong Chut King in 1900, the Centers for Disease Control and Prevention has counted approximately 1,000 cases in the United States. Most were bubonic plague.

About half of the cases occurred from 1900 to 1925. Nearly all of these were in port cities where international ships brought in infected fleas and rats. The United States has not had another epidemic of urban plague since 1924–25 in Los Angeles.

Before antibiotics, the death rate from all types of plague in the United States was 66 out of every 100 victims. During the past fifty years, thanks to these drugs, only about 13 percent of plague victims died, usually because they were not diagnosed correctly or treated quickly.

Today, an average of 7 people a year develop plague in America. The biggest threat is from the fleas of wild rodents in rural and

REPORTED CASES OF HUMAN PLAGUE—UNITED STATES, 1970–2012

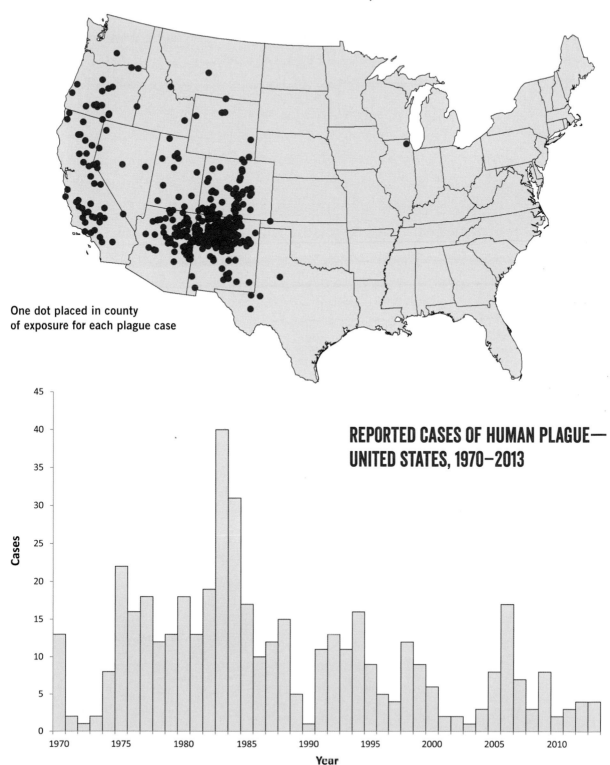

One dot placed in county
of exposure for each plague case

REPORTED CASES OF HUMAN PLAGUE—UNITED STATES, 1970–2013

semirural areas. Most of the cases occur in New Mexico, Arizona, Colorado, California, and southern Oregon. Victims are more likely to be infected during the late spring to early fall, when fleas and rodents are particularly active.

Anybody, no matter what age or gender, can be infected by Y. *pestis*. Yet about half the American cases are between the ages of twelve and forty-five. Today, this group tends to have more contact with wild animals and their fleas.

In 2002, a New Mexico couple, John and Lucinda, took a vacation in New York City. Early in their visit, they started to feel sick. For two days, they had high fever, chills, and aches. Then Lucinda felt a "painful, red-hot swelling" in her groin.

Because their illness seemed much worse than the flu, the couple went to a hospital to be checked. When the doctor spotted Lucinda's bubo, he knew exactly what was wrong, though he never expected to see plague in New York City.

Later the couple realized that infected fleas had probably bitten them during a hike in New Mexico shortly before their trip. They hadn't known that plague was a danger where they lived.

Doctors immediately gave them antibiotics to fight the infection. Ten days later, Lucinda had recovered and could leave the hospital. No one expected John to live.

Plague bacteria had invaded his bloodstream and lungs. He developed gangrene in his feet. Lucinda later wrote: "They were coal black. His toes looked so dry and brittle that I thought they would snap off if I touched them." Trying to save his life, doctors amputated John's feet. But his organs failed, and John was put on life support.

Miraculously, after nearly three months, he began to improve. He spent more than seven months in the hospital before he was well enough to go home.

CAT HAZARD

Some of the American plague cases of the past few decades
have originated with cats. Wild and domestic cats are extremely
susceptible to plague. Most are probably not infected by fleas but by
eating an infected rodent or rabbit. The bacteria may attack the cat's
body through the mucous membranes in its mouth. This is most
likely to happen when the membranes are scratched or cut or when
a sharp bone pierces them as the cat devours the infected animal.

When Y. *pestis* reaches the bloodstream and travels to the lungs,
the cat develops secondary pneumonic plague. If a human
breathes in infected droplets from the cat's sneeze or cough, he
or she may fall ill with primary pneumonic plague. In 1992, a
Colorado veterinarian died after an infected cat sneezed on him.

A pneumonic case from 2007 involved a wildlife biologist who
was studying mountain lions at Grand Canyon National Park in
Arizona. One day, he discovered the body of a big cat he'd been
tracking. The animal's chest wounds looked as if another lion had

Members of the cat family,
such as these mountain
lions, are particularly
susceptible to plague.

attacked it. To learn more, the biologist took the mountain lion home and performed an autopsy in his garage.

Three days later, the thirty-seven-year-old man felt feverish. He started coughing up sputum mixed with blood. He went to a doctor who diagnosed a common respiratory illness. A week after the mountain lion autopsy, the biologist was found dead. *Yersinia pestis* had invaded his body.

The mountain lion's body was infected, too. The biologist never suspected that plague killed the animal. He hadn't protected himself during the autopsy by wearing gloves or a face mask, and he probably breathed in infected droplets. Because the doctor had no idea that his patient might have been exposed to plague, he didn't test the man for the disease.

Bites and scratches have infected humans, too. A cat's claws and teeth may be covered with Y. *pestis* from its infected saliva or from a rodent it caught.

During the summer of 2012, a fifty-nine-year-old Oregon man named Paul noticed his cat Charlie choking on a dead mouse. When Paul tried to get the mouse from Charlie's jaws, the cat bit him.

Less than two days later, Paul suddenly started running a fever. He thought he had the flu, but he didn't get better. After Paul became delirious, he ended up in the hospital.

When doctors saw the lemon-sized lymph glands under his arms, they recognized bubonic plague. They put Paul on antibiotics.

The bacteria had already multiplied and spread too far, and Paul fell into critical condition. He developed all three types of plague: bubonic, septicemic, and pneumonic. His fingers and toes turned black, and doctors had to amputate them. He lay near death for a month, and doctors didn't expect him to make it.

Unlike his plague-infected cat, Paul survived, although he had to learn to live without his fingers and toes. His advice for others: "If you know the symptoms and what to look for, you stand a much better chance of surviving."

SLOWED, BUT NOT GONE

By the late 1920s, the Third Pandemic gradually subsided. The annual plague death rates in countries like India dropped to less than a tenth of what they had been in the first years of the pandemic. Plague's relentless spread into new places slowed down.

Since the 1850s, Y. *pestis* had raced around the world, killing at least 15 million people. About 2 million died in China. Densely populated India saw more than 12.5 million deaths.

Even though fewer people died across the globe than during the first two pandemics, plague spread farther. In just a few decades, Y. *pestis* reached every continent but Antarctica. It found a permanent home in the native rodents everywhere except Australia.

By the 1950s, doctors were using antibiotics to cure human plague victims. Researchers found cheaper, more effective poisons to kill rodents and fleas. As a result, the number of human cases and deaths dwindled.

REPORTED* PLAGUE CASES BY COUNTRY, 2000–2009

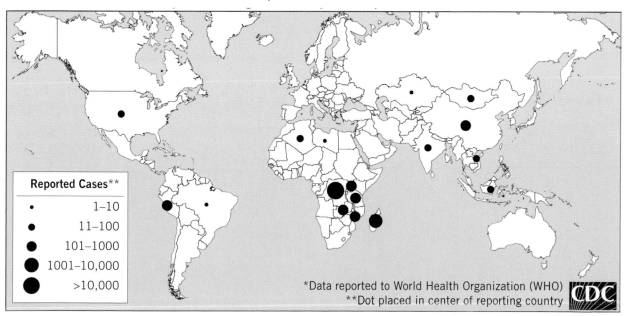

Reported Cases**
- · 1–10
- • 11–100
- ● 101–1000
- ● 1001–10,000
- ● >10,000

*Data reported to World Health Organization (WHO)
**Dot placed in center of reporting country

CDC

Today, 1,000 to 4,000 people throughout the world fall ill with plague each year, and about 200 of them die. The actual number varies from year to year and is undoubtedly higher. In many countries of Africa, Asia, and Latin America, plague isn't diagnosed or reported to authorities. Unless it's part of a large outbreak, an individual case might be overlooked.

More than 90 percent of cases are in Africa, mainly in Madagascar, Uganda, and the Democratic Republic of Congo. Most of the rest occur in central Asia, the Indian subcontinent, South America, and the southwestern United States.

Recent plague epidemics have occurred in communities where poverty, poor sanitation, and lack of rodent control create a fertile

PLAGUE CASES REPORTED TO THE WORLD HEALTH ORGANIZATION, 1954–2005, BY CONTINENTS

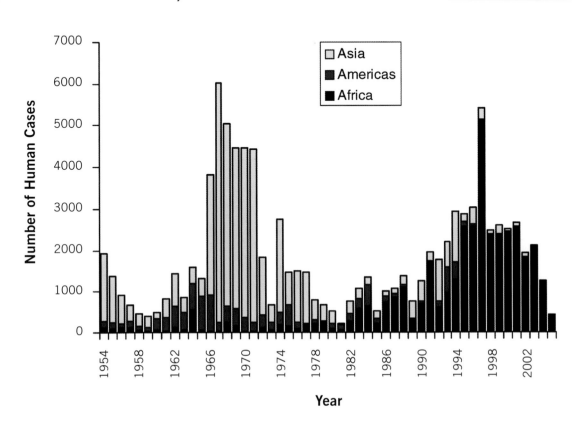

environment for infected fleas. In small villages and farming communities, people live close to rodents and are more vulnerable.

When a country has a weak healthcare system, victims aren't diagnosed and treated quickly enough to save their lives. Local officials may struggle to control fleas and rodents. If the disease spreads into an urban area, as has happened recently in Madagascar, the outbreak expands even faster.

BIOWEAPON

Y. *pestis* is considered so dangerous that federal law regulates its handling. It's potentially one of the most lethal bioweapons, along with anthrax, smallpox, and Ebola-like diseases.

According to fourteenth-century accounts, the Mongol army used plague as a bioweapon by catapulting their dead soldiers into Caffa. In fact, the infected fleas had likely left the corpses before they were flung over the walls. The disease probably entered Caffa with flea-infested rats scampering from the Mongol camp.

Six hundred years later, the Japanese used a plague weapon that worked better than catapulting dead bodies. During World War II, the Japanese filled pots with thousands of fleas that they had infected with Y. *pestis* in the laboratory. The fleas were combined with grain to attract rats and mice. Planes dropped the flea bombs onto several Chinese cities. Dozens of people on the ground developed bubonic plague, including more than 100 in a single city.

Even though no large epidemic broke out, as the Japanese had hoped, they decided to try again. In the summer of 1945, they planned to send kamikaze pilots to release swarms of infected fleas over San Diego, California. Fortunately, the war ended in August of that year, and the plot was never carried out.

During the Cold War of the 1950s–1980s, the United States and the Soviet Union studied plague as a potential weapon.

Security experts now worry that terrorists might release Y. *pestis* in an aerosol over a major city. As thousands of unsuspecting people breathed it in, their lungs would be infected. The resulting pneumonic plague could kill before victims were diagnosed and started on antibiotics. If the bacteria were manipulated in the laboratory to be antibiotic resistant, drugs wouldn't help. In the meantime, the first victims would spew contaminated droplets into the air with every cough, infecting many others.

The world's deadliest recorded pneumonic outbreak hints at how many people might die. In 1910, Chinese hunters traveled to Manchuria in northern Asia to gather valuable marmot skins. Local hunters always avoided colonies with sick animals, but the visitors weren't careful about ill or dead marmots. Plague-infected fleas in the pelts bit some of the men.

Bodies of plague victims are hauled away during the 1910–11 pneumonic plague outbreak in Manchuria.

Chinese authorities burn a plague-infected house.

When these hunters developed pneumonic plague, their coughs passed infected respiratory droplets to others in their crowded living quarters. Soon 600 people were dead. Other Chinese hunters panicked and fled the area in packed trains, spreading pneumonic plague to each other and to people at their destinations.

Chinese authorities finally contained the epidemic by restricting movement in the affected cities. They isolated victims and all their contacts. By the time the pneumonic outbreak ended five months later, plague had killed about 60,000 people. It started with just a few men.

A plague researcher in South Dakota marks an anesthetized prairie dog before releasing it back into the wild. The animal's hair and blood were tested.

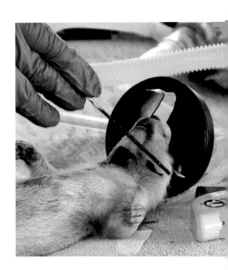

THE RESEARCH CONTINUES

Doctors and researchers know more about Y. *pestis* than their early twentieth-century predecessors did. Yet secrets remain, and many teams of scientists are working to uncover them.

Some researchers are trying to understand how Y. *pestis* overpowers the human immune system and infects the body. That may provide clues to better treatments. By studying the bacterium's genome, scientists hope to discover faster tests to detect plague and more effective drugs to cure it. A constant worry is that Y. *pestis* will become resistant to current antibiotics.

These advancements could also lead to a reliable and safe vaccine. Currently in the United States, there is no commercially available plague vaccine.

Biologists are testing an oral vaccine put in bait around prairie dog colonies. If it works at controlling plague outbreaks in these animals, it could be used on urban rats.

Through the ages, *Yersinia pestis* caused tens of millions of people to suffer a cruel, agonizing death. Today, it's less likely that a few plague cases will turn into a pandemic that sweeps the world.

But the lethal microbe hasn't gone away. And no one knows when or where the phantom killer will strike again.

The reddish peanut-butter-flavored bait next to this prairie dog burrow contains a trial plague vaccine.

PLAGUE FREQUENTLY ASKED QUESTIONS

HOW CAN I AVOID GETTING PLAGUE?

Be aware if you live or visit anywhere plague has been detected in wild animals. Officials post warnings in public parks when they find a plague-infected animal, sometimes even closing the park for a time.

Don't touch or go near wild rodents and rabbits, particularly sick and dying ones. Infected fleas may jump from a dead animal onto you or your pet. If you're hiking, use insect repellent on your pants and shoes.

Cats, and occasionally dogs, can get plague by hunting or eating infected animals. Don't let your pets roam where plague might exist. Control their fleas, because pets can bring the insects into your house, putting you and your family at risk.

If you hunt or trap, protect your hands and face when skinning wild animals.

Plague bacteria can be destroyed by high temperatures, chlorine, and other disinfectants.

Prairie dogs are highly susceptible to plague.

WHAT WILL HAPPEN TO ME IF I GET PLAGUE?

To have the best chance of recovering, you must receive the correct antibiotic before the disease ravages your body. Once the bacteria infect your blood, drugs may not be able to stop them.

If you have pneumonic plague, you must get antibiotics on the day you first show symptoms. Without that rapid treatment, you'll have a slim chance of surviving.

Because many different diseases start with fever, achiness, or cough, your medical provider might not suspect plague, especially if you don't have a bubo. That's why your life depends on your telling him or her right away whether you have possibly been exposed to a plague-infected animal or its fleas.

A colony of *Yersinia pestis* appears white as it grows on a preparation of sheep's blood in a petri dish.

If a doctor thinks you might have plague, he or she is required to report it to local and state health departments. Laboratory tests will check for plague using samples from your lymph nodes, blood, or sputum. Medical staff will look for *Y. pestis* under a microscope. They will culture the sample and observe the way the bacteria grow, analyze the microbe's biochemistry, or use other tests to determine if you're infected.

However, your doctor won't wait for the lab results. You'll get antibiotics immediately. If you have plague, every minute matters.

If you're suspected of being infected, you'll be put in isolation until you finish forty-eight hours of antibiotic treatment and your condition improves. Healthcare workers take special precautions around people who develop pneumonic plague to avoid being infected by contaminated respiratory droplets. Everyone who has had close contact with a pneumonic plague victim, and is still healthy, is given antibiotics and monitored for fever or cough.

The health department will investigate how you were exposed to *Y. pestis* in order to prevent that source from infecting others.

WHY DID ONLY ABOUT 200 PEOPLE DIE IN THE SAN FRANCISCO OUTBREAKS COMPARED WITH MILLIONS IN CHINA AND INDIA DURING THE SAME PERIOD?

The actual number of deaths in San Francisco was probably higher than officials counted. Even so, the total never approached the Asian epidemics.

Fewer people in San Francisco were exposed to plague than in the congested cities of China and India. The extensive cleanup of Chinatown reduced the rat habitats (and, therefore, the fleas) around homes and businesses. During the outbreak after the earthquake, rat eradication and rat-proofing lowered the plague risk to humans.

When the Marine-Hospital Service examined rat fleas in the early 1900s, researchers found that only about 20 percent were *Xenopsylla cheopis*, the species infesting rats in Asia. The other fleas on San Francisco's rats were less effective at transmitting plague. This could have affected how far and how fast plague spread.

FASTEN THIS UP IN YOUR KITCHEN.

Citizens' Health Committee,
Headquarters, Room 1233 Merchants' Exchange.

TO GET RID OF RATS.

KITCHEN RULES.

Keep all supplies in rat-proof bins.
Keep meats in safes or in refrigerators.
Keep uncooked vegetables in crates on shelves. Never on the floor.

IF COOKING IS DONE WITH A COAL FIRE.

Burn in your kitchen fire all refuse (trimmings of meat, bones, parings of vegetables, egg shells, all platter and plate scrapings, and all waste food) as it occurs. This means the putting into the fire of small amounts at a time, when they will readily burn. This is known to be a practical method. By it there is no garbage.

IF COOKING IS DONE WITH A GAS FIRE.

Keep all garbage in covered metal cans.
Keep the cans closely covered.
Have the garbage removed at least twice a week.
Have scavenger carry your garbage can to his wagon.
Report all scavengers who do not do so.
Don't put garbage in slop hoppers.
Always clean up your own premises.
Throw no garbage into the street nor on vacant lots.
Admit authorized Health Inspectors to your premises. They are there for your benefit.
Tell your neighbors to do all the above—and see that they do.
Report to the Committee all cases of insanitary conditions.
These rules to be in force during the existence of plague and afterwards.

WHY DID THE FIRST AND SECOND PANDEMICS END?

No one knows, though scientists and historians have several possible explanations. Changes in weather and climate might have affected *Y. pestis* and its mammal and flea hosts. Rodent populations could have decreased in certain areas of the world, lowering the chances of human contact with infected fleas.

As geneticists, microbiologists, and historians gather more evidence, our understanding of plague and its history might change.

ABOVE: A flyer tells San Franciscans how to keep food away from rats.

BELOW: Scientists think *Y. pestis* evolved to be a dangerous microbe sometime between 1,500 and 10,000 years ago.

COULD A DISEASE OTHER THAN PLAGUE HAVE CAUSED THE BLACK DEATH?

A few researchers claim that a different disease, such as anthrax or an Ebola-like illness, killed the tens of millions of Black Death victims. Most plague experts don't agree with that idea because the symptoms described in historical writings match those of today's plague patients. The majority of victims from the First and Second Pandemics likely had the bubonic type. A smaller group might have developed septicemic and pneumonic plague.

In several recent studies, researchers examined the remains of people buried in Europe's plague graves during the Second Pandemic. Scientists found evidence of *Yersinia pestis* in the pulp of the victims' teeth. This supports the view that plague swept the world during the Black Death.

IF PLAGUE CAUSED THE BLACK DEATH, WHY DID SO MANY MORE PEOPLE DIE THEN COMPARED WITH TODAY?

Some have argued that a more lethal strain of *Y. pestis* infected people. Different strains do exist, and scientists are debating exactly how many. But DNA found in the teeth of Second Pandemic plague victims indicates that the infecting strain was probably the same one around today.

One hypothesis for the higher death rates is that people living during the First and Second Pandemics were genetically more susceptible to *Y. pestis*. Another possible explanation is that more victims developed pneumonic plague. Some experts have proposed that human, not rat, fleas helped transmit plague rapidly among people living close together in small huts and cottages.

Without more evidence, none of these ideas can be confirmed.

The lower fatality rates today are related to important changes in how public health officials and physicians handle plague.

During the first two pandemics, many people lived in buildings that were easy for rodents to enter. Thatched roofs harbored rats. Grain was stored near or in

Rats are attracted to grains. Plague might have spread quickly during the First and Second Pandemics because people stored food close to their living quarters.

homes. Rodents thrived, leading to a high number of human plague victims.

In the twentieth century, health officials learned how to prevent plague's spread. They stopped rodents from getting access to food and nesting areas. They used poisons to kill them and insecticides to wipe out their fleas.

The 1894 discovery of the plague bacterium helped researchers find treatments. Even though the Yersin serum and Haffkine vaccine had serious drawbacks, they reduced the number of victims during the early 1900s. When antibiotics became available in the 1940s, the death rate from plague plunged.

A shirt used to educate the people of Uganda about the signs of plague. Today, Africa has more cases of human plague than any other continent.

Today, epidemics periodically occur in parts of the world where living conditions bring humans in contact with infected rodents and fleas. *Y. pestis* may still be moving into new areas. But the number of plague victims is small compared with earlier times.

171

GLOSSARY

Antibiotic: a drug used to destroy disease-causing bacteria.

Antibody: a protein produced by the body in response to the presence of an antigen, which the antibody binds to and neutralizes.

Antigen: a substance foreign to the body, such as a microbe or poison.

Bacilli: rod-shaped bacteria.

Bacteria: microscopic one-celled organisms.

Bacteriologist: a scientist who studies bacteria.

Bioweapon: biological material, such as dangerous microbes, used in warfare or terrorism.

Black Death: the name later given to the well-known bubonic plague in fourteenth-century Europe.

Bubo: a painful swelling of a lymph node, often in the armpit or groin, seen in bubonic plague.

Cholera: a deadly infectious disease with symptoms of extreme vomiting and diarrhea, caused by a bacterium.

Contagious disease: an illness spread by contact between animals.

Culture: to grow bacteria in a special nutrient-containing gel or liquid; the colony of bacteria that grows this way.

Diphtheria: a contagious and sometimes fatal upper-respiratory disease caused by a bacterium.

Entomologist: a scientist who studies insects.

Epidemic: a disease that spreads to many members of a population at the same time.

Gangrene: death of body tissue caused by an inadequate blood supply.

Genome: an organism's genetic material.

Germ theory: the idea that diseases can be caused by microorganisms.

Groin: the area of the body where thigh and abdomen meet.

Infectious disease: an illness caused by an organism such as a bacterium, virus, or parasite that invades the body.

Isolation: separation of people sick with a contagious disease from those who aren't ill.

Lymph node or gland: a small mass of tissue that is part of the body's disease-fighting system.

Microbe (or microorganism): a microscopic organism, such as a bacterium or virus.

Pandemic: a disease epidemic that spreads over an extensive area, such as continents or the entire world.

Pesthouse: a building used to isolate plague victims.

Pharynx: the area between the mouth and nasal passages and the esophagus.

Pneumonic plague: a form of plague in which the lungs are infected.

Quarantine: forced separation of people suspected of exposure to a contagious disease from the rest of the population in order to prevent the disease's spread.

Rabies: an infectious, deadly disease of the nervous system caused by a virus.

Septicemic plague: a form of plague in which the blood is infected.

Serum: the clear, yellowish liquid component of blood.

Smallpox: an often fatal contagious disease caused by a virus. Symptoms include high fever and skin sores.

Sputum: phlegm and mucus coughed up from the lungs by pneumonic plague victims.

Toxin: a poison, such as one produced by a microbe.

Tuberculosis: a serious and sometimes fatal lung disease caused by a bacterium.

Typhoid fever: an infectious disease caused by a bacterium that spreads through food and water contaminated with body waste.

Typhus: an infectious disease caused by a bacterium that is transmitted by fleas, lice, mites, and ticks.

Vaccine: a special preparation of killed or weakened microbes that triggers the body to produce immunity to a disease.

Vector: an organism, often an insect, that transports a disease-causing microbe from one animal (or person) to another.

Venereal disease: a sexually transmitted disease.

TIMELINE

541–750?	1346?–EARLY 18TH CENTURY	1346–53	1850s
First [Justinian] Pandemic.	Second Pandemic.	Black Death.	Third Pandemic begins.

New California governor takes office.

1904	1903	1901
February — Last death in first San Francisco epidemic.	Rupert Blue leads new plague campaign.	**February —** Federal plague commission investigation launched in San Francisco.
		April — Kinyoun transferred from San Francisco.

1906	1907
April 18 — San Francisco earthquake.	**May —** First death in second San Francisco plague epidemic.
	September — Blue returns to San Francisco to head anti-plague efforts.

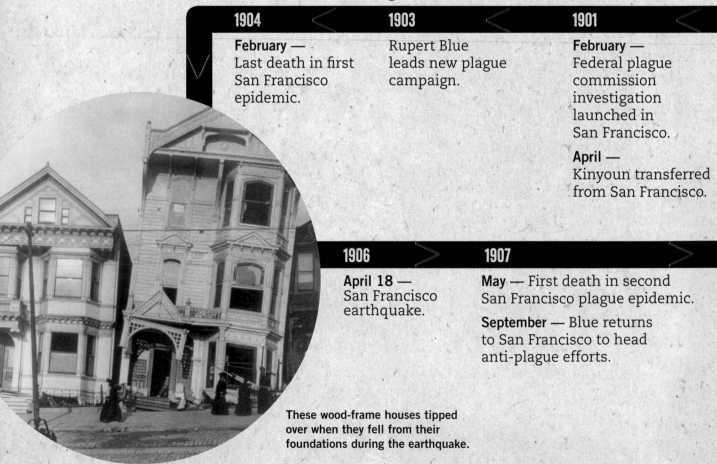

These wood-frame houses tipped over when they fell from their foundations during the earthquake.

Plague epidemics
in Canton and
Hong Kong.

Plague epidemics
begin in India.

Yersin develops
anti-plague serum.

1894

1896

1897

1898

June 20 —
Alexandre Yersin
identifies plague
bacterium.

Waldemar Haffkine
develops plague
vaccine.

Masanori Ogata
finds plague
bacteria in fleas.

Paul-Louis Simond
proves that fleas
transmit plague
bacteria.

1900

March 6 —
Wong Chut King dies
in Chinatown, San Francisco.

March 7–9 — Board of Health
quarantines Chinatown.

March 13 — Joseph Kinyoun
confirms first U.S. case of plague.

May 29–June 15 —
Second Chinatown quarantine.

Two children walk alone in Chinatown, around
1900. Chinese leaders declared that the
second quarantine did more harm than good.

1899

Plague epidemic
begins in
Honolulu.

1908

1924–25

1934

1940s

February — Last death
from second San
Francisco epidemic.

July — Plague-infected
ground squirrels
confirmed in
California.

Human pneumonic
plague epidemic in
Los Angeles.

Plague-infected
wild rodents found
outside California.

Antibiotics
and insecticides
developed to fight
plague.

FOR MORE INFORMATION*

ON PLAGUE

"Plague."
Centers for Disease Control and Prevention.
cdc.gov/plague/
 The site provides an extensive source of information about the disease and its history, a fact sheet, a podcast about plague in the United States since 1900, and tips for avoiding plague. It includes links to additional resources.

"Emergency Preparedness and Response."
Centers for Disease Control and Prevention.
www.bt.cdc.gov/agent/plague/trainingmodule/index.asp
 The CDC learning module includes photographs, facts, and discussion about plague diagnosis and treatment.

Plague by Rachel C. Abbott and Tonie E. Rocke.
U.S. Geological Survey, Circular 1372, National Wildlife Health Center.
pubs.usgs.gov/circ/1372/
 This report on plague was prepared for the general public. It includes scientific background on the disease, discussion of its cycle in nature, a list of susceptible animals, and the disease's current status in the United States.

*Websites active at time of publication

"Plague."
National Institute of Allergy and Infectious Diseases.
www.niaid.nih.gov/topics/plague/Pages/Default.aspx

The website includes basic information about plague's transmission, symptoms, and treatment. It discusses the current research to develop effective vaccines, diagnostic tests, and drug treatments.

"Plague."
World Health Organization.
who.int/topics/plague/en/

Find links to a plague fact sheet, technical information and publications about the disease, and updates on recent outbreaks.

ON THE BLACK DEATH

"The Past, Present and Future of the Bubonic Plague" by Sharon N. DeWitte. TED-Ed.
ed.ted.com/lessons/the-past-present-and-future-of-the-bubonic-plague-sharon-n-dewitte

Watch this short illustrated TED-Ed talk for students, presented by a researcher who studies the Black Death. A video discusses the causes and effects of the epidemic and presents possible explanations for plague's high death rate during the fourteenth century. Site contains a short quiz and discussion questions. Links connect to articles and other TED-Ed videos about plague, pandemics, and quarantine.

The Black Death. Written, produced, and directed by Peter Nicholson for Channel 4/Granada Television, 2004.
Also available on YouTube.
youtube.com/watch?v=-fAhOVFp54E

This documentary dramatically examines the Black Death in Europe, from 1348 to 1350.

ON THE SAN FRANCISCO PLAGUE

The Barbary Plague: The Black Death in Victorian San Francisco by Marilyn Chase. New York: Random House, 2003.

Plague, Fear, and Politics in San Francisco's Chinatown by Guenter B. Risse. Baltimore: Johns Hopkins University Press, 2012.

These two adult nonfiction books examine the people and politics involved in the San Francisco plague outbreaks, taking the story beyond the scope of *Bubonic Panic*.

"Dr. Joseph J. Kinyoun: Father of the NIH."
National Institute of Allergy and Infectious Diseases.
www.niaid.nih.gov/about/whoweare/history/josephjkinyoun/Pages/default.aspx

Watch a video, listen to a podcast, and read the short book, *The Indispensable Forgotten Man* by David M. Morens; Victoria A. Harden; Joseph Kinyoun Houts, Jr.; and Anthony S. Fauci, about Kinyoun's life and work in public service.

ON THE 1906 EARTHQUAKE

"The Great 1906 Earthquake and Fire."
The Virtual Museum of the City of San Francisco.
sfmuseum.net/1906/06.html

This site includes photographs, a timeline, newspaper clippings, and eyewitness accounts of the earthquake.

"The Great 1906 San Francisco Earthquake."
United States Geological Survey.
earthquake.usgs.gov/regional/nca/1906/18april/

See photos of the devastation and learn about the science behind the quake.

Before and After the Great Earthquake and Fire: Early Films of
San Francisco, 1897–1916.
Library of Congress.
loc.gov/collections/san-francisco-earthquake-and-fire-1897-to-1916/?sp=2

    View short silent films taken in San Francisco at the turn of the
twentieth century. The films show scenes of San Francisco before the
1906 earthquake, including a street in Chinatown in 1900 during the
plague crisis and footage taken from a hydrogen balloon in 1902. Also
watch films of the destroyed buildings and refugee camps during the
earthquake's aftermath. A commentary accompanies each clip.

ON CHINESE IMMIGRATION

Angel Island: Gateway to Gold Mountain by Russell Freedman. New York:
Clarion Books, 2013.

    This nonfiction book gives an overview of the problems faced
by Chinese immigrants in California starting in the early 1850s.
It describes Angel Island after 1910, when the island became an
immigration station for arrivals from Asia.

The Chinese in America, 1850–1925.
American Memory, Library of Congress.
memory.loc.gov:8081/ammem/award99/cubhtml/themeindex.html

The Bancroft Library.
bancroft.berkeley.edu/collections/chineseinca/index.html

    These two connected websites include photographs, manuscripts,
documents, and commentary about the Chinese and Chinese
American experience in California.

AUTHOR'S NOTE

Bubonic Panic is the final book in my Deadly Diseases trilogy, preceded by *Red Madness: How a Medical Mystery Changed What We Eat* and *Fatal Fever: Tracking Down Typhoid Mary*. Before I began my research into plague, I thought this would be the topic about which I already knew the most. I was surprised at what I didn't know—what no one knows—about this mysterious disease.

By reading the scholarly books and articles listed in the Bibliography (page 188), I learned more about the first two pandemics, the early bacteriological discoveries, and the arrival of plague in the United States.

For firsthand accounts of San Francisco's two outbreaks, I used early twentieth-century medical journals, newspapers, and eyewitness reports. Invaluable sources were the *Annual Report of the Surgeon General* and the weekly *Public Health Reports* published during the early 1900s. These included telegrams between Surgeon General Walter Wyman and his medical officers, revealing the opinions, plans, and actions of the Marine-Hospital Service (later known as the Public Health Service). All direct quotations in the book come from primary sources and are cited in the Source Notes (page 182).

Nature and man have changed the appearance of San Francisco's Chinatown since plague's arrival. But the images and commentary in *Genthe's Photographs of San Francisco's Old Chinatown* (Arnold Genthe and John Kuo Wei Tchen) gave me a sense of the neighborhood and its people from 1900 to 1906. The rare film clips from the Library of Congress (on the website Before and After the Great Earthquake and Fire: Early Films of San Francisco, 1897–1916) helped bring the city to life for me.

To familiarize myself with current scientific knowledge, I read medical journals and books and interviewed researchers. From talking with Dr. Kenneth Gage of the Centers for Disease Control and Prevention and attending a lecture by Dr. B. Joseph Hinnebusch of the National Institute of Allergy and Infectious Diseases, I realized that the understanding of plague is constantly evolving. Many aspects of the relationships between plague bacteria, fleas, and host mammals remain to be studied. In fact, the changes are coming so fast that before this book went into production, I had to rewrite a section to reflect newly published research about *Yersinia pestis*'s invasion of the mammal body.

While I worked on *Bubonic Panic*, I used a news alert to keep up on recent plague cases in the United States and the world. Those cases included a serious outbreak of bubonic plague in Madagascar as well as the first American pneumonic plague outbreak since 1924–25. Plague will likely continue to make the headlines in the future.

The early 1900s was an important and exciting era of medicine wedged between the discovery of disease-causing microbes in the late 1800s and the development of antibiotics in the 1940s. Scientists, physicians, and public health officials worked together to unlock the secrets of human illnesses and answer the questions: What causes diseases? How can we stop their spread? How can we treat and cure the sick?

As I've written this trilogy, my admiration has grown for the men and women who devoted their lives to public health. They occasionally made mistakes in judgment. Their actions sometimes revealed strong egos and ambition. Yet they acted not for reward of money and power but to save lives.

The story of plague's invasion of America is more than a tale about an ancient disease threatening a modern society. It's also about the tensions between old, faulty assumptions and fresh scientific insights; between local and federal governments; between people living inside and outside an infected area; and between individual rights and a community's welfare.

History can show us how to deal with these inevitable tensions *when*—not *if*—we have to fight another frightening deadly disease spreading around the globe. The response to the recent Ebola crisis shows that the world might not yet be ready for this battle.

—GJ
December 2015

SOURCE NOTES*

The source of each quotation in this book is found below. The citation indicates the first words of the quotation and its document source. The sources are listed either in the bibliography or below.

The following abbreviations are used:

SF Call — San Francisco Call

SG — Annual Report of the Supervising Surgeon-General of the Marine-Hospital Service/Surgeon-General of the Public Health and Marine-Hospital Service/ Surgeon General of the Public Health Service of the United States

CHAPTER ONE • PHANTOM KILLER (PAGE 8)
"We see death . . .": Gethin, quoted in Mike Ibeji, "Black Death," History, BBC, March 10, 2011, bbc.co.uk/history/british/middle_ages/black_01.shtml.

CHAPTER TWO • PANDEMIC! (PAGE 12)
"This is the end . . .": di Tura, *Cronica Sanese*, 1348, quoted in Langton Douglas, *A History of Siena*, London: John Murray, 1902, p. 150.
"the whole human . . .": Procopius, *History of the Wars, Book 2*, translated by H. B. Dewing, Cambridge, MA: Harvard University Press, 1914, p. 362.
"bubonic . . ." and "a deep coma . . .": same as above, p. 367.
"crying out . . .": same as above, p. 368.
"pestilence.": same as above, p. 362.
"an evil stench . . .": same as above, p. 374.
"It embraced . . .": same as above, p. 363.
"The sailors . . .": quoted in "The Plague at Hong Kong," *Lancet*, June 23, 1894, p. 1581.
"Many died of boils . . .": Clyn, *The Annals of Ireland*, edited by the Very Reverend Richard Butler, Dublin: Irish Archaeological Society, 1849, p. vi.
"It is seething . . .": Gethin, quoted in Mike Ibeji, "Black Death," History, BBC, March 10, 2011.
"Very wide . . .": di Tura, *Cronica Sanese*, 1348, quoted in Langton Douglas, *A History of Siena*.
"Men shrank . . .": *John of Fordun's Chronicle of the Scottish Nation*, edited by William F. Skene, Edinburgh: Edmonston and Douglas, 1872, p. 359.

*Websites active at time of publication

CHAPTER THREE • RETURN OF THE SCOURGE (PAGE 24)

"The Chinese are not . . .": "The Late Outbreak of Bubonic
Plague at Hong-Kong," *Lancet*, November 24, 1894, p. 1234.

"Rats in infected . . .": Niles, quoted in W. J. Simpson, *A Treatise on Plague Dealing
with the Historical, Epidemiological, Clinical, Therapeutic and Preventive
Aspects of the Disease*, Cambridge: Cambridge University Press, 1905, p. 61.

"That there is . . .": "The Plague at Hong Kong," *Lancet*, June 23, 1894, p. 1582.

"highly contagious": same as above, p. 1581.

"The houses . . .": S. Kitasato, "The Bacillus of Bubonic Plague," *Lancet*,
August 25, 1894, p. 430.

"It is a disease . . .": Surgeon General W. K. Van Reypen of the U.S. Navy, quoted
in "Police Keeping Quarantine Guard Over Chinatown," *SF Call*, March 7, 1900.

CHAPTER FOUR • SECRETS UNCOVERED (PAGE 32)

"I go on cutting . . .": Yersin diary, June 21, 1894, quoted in Gregg, p. 53.

"To ask for money . . .": letter from Yersin to mother, 1891, same as above, p. 54.

"The first thing . . .": Yersin, quoted in Marriott, p. 38.

"More than anything . . .": Yersin, same as above, p. 118.

"I am surprised . . .": Yersin, same as above, p. 98.

"The specimen is . . ." and "This is without . . .": Yersin notebook, June 20, 1894,
quoted in Gross, p. 7610.

"My animals inoculated . . .": Yersin diary, June 21, 1894, quoted in Gregg, p. 53.

"The microbe . . .": letter from Yersin to Pasteur Institute, quoted in Marriott, p. 144.

"I salute you . . .": letter from Lowson to Kitasato, August 20, 1894, in Marriott.

"Plague is . . .": Yersin, "La Peste Bubonique à Hong-Kong," *Annales de l'Institut
Pasteur*, 1894, p. 664, quoted in Echenberg, *Plague Ports*, p. 6.

"All through . . .": Wyman, SG 1897, p. 413.

CHAPTER FIVE • INJECTIONS OF HOPE (PAGE 41)

"People . . . in Bombay . . .": "To the editor of the *Times of India*," by J. G. D'Souza,
Times of India, January 13, 1897.

"Every one . . .": "Plague-Stricken Bombay," by M. A. M., *Good Words*, December 1899,
p. 842.

"All round one . . .": same as above, p. 843.

"Sometimes we think . . .": same as above, p. 844.

"My temperature . . .": Haffkine, quoted in "Professor Haffkine in London,"
Times of India, May 18, 1899.

"The benefits . . .": same as above.

CHAPTER SIX • FLEAS AND FLAMES (PAGE 50)

"Modern quarantine . . .": Wyman, *The Bubonic Plague*, p. 31.

"We have to assume . . .": Simond, quoted in Gross, p. 7610.

"abundant plague . . .": Simond, quoted in Marriott, p. 242.

"I felt an . . .": same as above.

"One should pay . . .": Ogata, quoted in Gregg, p. 58.

"The epidemic . . .": Wyman, *The Bubonic Plague*, p. 4.

CHAPTER SEVEN · DEATH IN CHINATOWN (PAGE 62)

"The existence . . .": Kellogg, "Report of the Bacteriologist," July 1, 1900, in
    Biennial Report of the Board of Health, p. 144.
"I have reason . . .": Kellogg, quoted in "Bubonic Plague Case," *Los Angeles Times*,
    March 8, 1900.
"Feeding Ground": O'Brien, quoted in "Board of Health Discusses the Chinatown
    Quarantine," *SF Call*, March 8, 1900.
"a magnificent . . .": same as above.
"the ashes will . . .": "Burning of Dead Body," *Chung Sai Yat Po*, March 21, 1900,
    quoted in Chase, p. 19.
"outrageous . . .": Ho, quoted in "Consul Utters Veiled Threat," *SF Call*, March 8, 1900.
"remove the ban . . .": same as above.
"a sham . . .": "Sanitary Politics," *SF Call*, March 9, 1900.
"the purpose of . . .": *San Francisco Evening Post*, March 7, 1900, republished in
    "Quarantine in 'Frisco," *Honolulu Star*, March 15, 1900.
"sensational statement . . ." and "The bubonic plague fake" and "The most
    dangerous . . ." and "a plague of . . . ": "Plague Fake Part of Plot to Plunder,"
    SF Call, March 8, 1900.
"a scientific . . ." and "on the testimony . . .": "The Bubonic Board," *SF Call*,
    March 11, 1900.
"international . . .": Ho, quoted in "Plague Farce Over and Health Board Quits
    the Stage," *SF Call*, March 10, 1900.

CHAPTER EIGHT · THE MONKEY DIED (PAGE 76)

"An epidemic . . .": Wyman, SG 1901, p. 539.
"Completed examination . . .": telegram from Kinyoun to Wyman, March 11, 1900,
    SG 1900, p. 532.
"Make following . . ." and "sufficient for . . .": telegram from Wyman to Gassaway,
    March 8, 1900, SG 1900, p. 531.
"There is not . . .": "Editorial," *Pacific Medical Journal*, April 1900, p. 292.
"a ruse . . ." and "the outrageous acts . . .": Ho, quoted in "Bubonic in San Francisco,"
    Washington Post, March 13, 1900.
"organism very . . .": telegram from Kinyoun to Wyman, March 19, 1900, SG 1900,
    p. 533.
"Expect there . . .": telegram from Kinyoun to Wyman, March 23, 1900, SG 1900, p. 535.
"There is no use . . .": Williamson, quoted in SG 1900, p. 534.
"The whole neighborhood . . .": same as above.
"Health Board . . .": untitled, *SF Call*, March 23, 1900.
"The Black Plague . . .": *New York Journal*, quoted in "The Yellow Plague," *SF Call*,
    March 25, 1900.
"Tourists Fleeing . . .": *Denver Republican*, quoted in "Another Glaring Effect of
    Mr. Hearst's Yellow Journalism," *SF Call*, March 28, 1900.
"will require . . .": telegram from Kinyoun to Wyman, May 15, 1900, SG 1900, p. 537.
"Over 35,000 . . ." and "depopulation": same as above.
"Bubonic Horror . . .": "Fighting the Plague," [Washington, D.C.] *Times*, May 20, 1900.
"Dread Plague": *Indianapolis* [IN] *Journal*, May 20, 1900.
"there has been . . .": "Another Plague Scare," *SF Call*, May 22, 1900.
"Can you . . .": "Submit Proofs or Retract," *SF Call*, May 24, 1900.

"a well developed . . .": "Another Plague Scare," *SF Call*, May 22, 1900.

"People here . . .": telegram from Kinyoun to Wyman, May 20, 1900, SG 1900, p. 541.

"In my opinion . . .": telegram from Kinyoun to Wyman, May 19, 1900, SG 1900, p. 540.

"Allow no Chinese . . .": telegram from Wyman to Kinyoun, May 19, 1900, SG 1900, p. 541.

"been treated with . . ." and "rudely . . .": "Japanese Lodge Complaint," *Washington Post*, June 1, 1900.

"The health board . . .": Ho, quoted in "Fighting the Plague," [Washington, D.C.] *Times*, May 20, 1900.

"the 25,000 . . ." and "There is not . . .": opinion in *Wong Wai v. John M. Williamson, et al.*, SG 1900, p. 553.

"a large exodus . . ." and "situation to . . .": telegram from Kinyoun to Wyman, May 28, 1900, SG 1900, p. 549.

CHAPTER NINE · QUARANTINE OUTRAGE (PAGE 90)

"It is unreasonable . . .": opinion in *Jew Ho v. John M. Williamson, et al.*, SG 1900, p. 597.

"necessary to prevent . . .": ordinance by Board of Supervisors, May 28, 1900, SG 1900, p. 587.

"a menace to . . ." and "aliens, who . . .": W. S. Chalmers, "Report of the Chief Sanitary Inspector," July 1, 1900, *Biennial Report of the Board of Health*, p. 74.

"without doubt . . .": "Plague Precaution—Physicians Urge the Necessity of Killing Rats," *Public Health Reports*, March 16, 1900.

"Do they want . . .": Ho, quoted in "Officials Investigating the Chinese Blackmail Scandal," *SF Call*, June 10, 1900.

"No white man . . ." and "That is . . .": "The Farcical Side of It," *SF Call*, May 30, 1900.

"Bubonic plague . . .": telegram from Gage to Secretary of State John Hay, June 13, 1900, quoted in "State Executive's Findings," *SF Call*, June 14, 1900.

"appalling . . .": "Sister States Have No Reason for Fear," by George F. Shrady, *SF Call*, June 1, 1900.

"I would advocate . . .": D. D. Crowley, quoted in "Dr. Crowley Would Burn Down Chinatown," *SF Call*, May 31, 1900.

"never has been . . .": opinion in *Jew Ho v. John M. Williamson, et al.*, SG 1900, p. 588.

"is made to operate . . .": same as above, p. 595.

"It is unreasonable . . .": same as above, p. 597.

"unless ordered . . .": telegram from Kinyoun to Wyman, June 16, 1900, SG 1900, p. 565.

"Perhaps some inadvertently . . .": "California Up In Arms Against the Kinyoun Quarantine Outrage," *SF Call*, June 18, 1900.

"the removal . . ." and "The harm . . .": "Kinyoun's Quarantine Outrage," *SF Call*, June 18, 1900.

"Withdraw all . . .": telegram from Wyman to Kinyoun, June 18, 1900, SG 1900, p. 566.

"Kinyoun did not . . .": opinion in *Wong Wai v. John M. Williamson, et al.*, SG 1900, p. 606.

"I am at war . . .": letter from Kinyoun to Dr. Preston H. Bailhache, quoted in Chase, p. 79.

CHAPTER TEN · NO END IN SIGHT (PAGE 100)

"Eradicate this . . .": letter from Kinyoun to Wyman, December 6, 1900, *SG* 1901, p. 499.

"that the mild . . .": same as above, p. 497.

"The sanitary . . .": same as above.

"plague will exist . . .": same as above, p. 499.

"a felony punishable . . .": "Gage Reviews State Needs," *Los Angeles Times*, January 9, 1901.

"Dr. J. J. Kinyoun . . .": "Solons Ready for Business," *Los Angeles Times*, January 9, 1901.

"to slander the fair . . ." and "man of black . . ." and "deserved to be . . .": Senator Cutter, quoted in "Kinyoun Skinned in the Senate," *Los Angeles Times*, January 24, 1901.

"I [am] being . . .": telegram from Kinyoun to Wyman, January 10, 1901, *SG* 1901, p. 503.

"youthful and . . .": *San Francisco Bulletin*, January 29, 1901, quoted in Kalisch, p. 128.

"The newspapers . . .": letter from Frederick Novy to Grace Novy, February 4, 1901, quoted in Kazanjian, p. 1375.

"[We] conclude . . .": Simon Flexner, F. G. Novy, and Lewellys F. Barker, "Report of the Commission," February 26, 1901, *SG* 1901, p. 525.

"Every pathologist . . .": Barker in *Transactions*, p. 520.

"will not try . . .": telegram from Kinyoun to Wyman, March 1, 1901, *SG* 1901, p. 523.

"brutally maligned . . .": John M. Williamson, *Annual Report of the Department of Public Health of San Francisco*, 1901, p. 14.

"had fearlessly . . .": minority report of the California Assembly Committee on Federal Relations, quoted in "Removal of Kinyoun," *Los Angeles Times*, February 6, 1901.

"the most disgraceful . . .": "The Governor's Message and the Plague," *Occidental Medical Times*, February 1901, p. 60.

CHAPTER ELEVEN · CHANGES AT THE TOP (PAGE 108)

"Rats Must Go": "Protection from Plague," *Los Angeles Times*, January 8, 1903.

"ignorance and . . ." and "inaccurate reports . . .": Gage, quoted in "Splenetic Farewell to Public Life," *Los Angeles Times*, January 7, 1903.

"If the whole thing . . .": W. W. Beckett, quoted in "Protection from Plague," *Los Angeles Times*, January 8, 1903.

"that all danger . . .": "Resolutions of Mercantile Joint Committee," February 2, 1903, *SG* 1903, p. 244.

"eradicating plague . . .": "Plague," *SG* 1905, p. 162.

CHAPTER TWELVE · EARTHQUAKE! (PAGE 119)

"Frisco . . .": *Guthrie [OK] Daily Leader*, April 18, 1906.

"Stricken San Francisco . . .": *Bemidji [MN] Daily Pioneer*, April 19, 1906.

"The City of . . .": *Evening Times [Grand Forks, ND]*, April 19, 1906.

"assume immediate . . .": mayor of San Francisco, quoted in telegram from President Theodore Roosevelt to Wyman, September 5, 1907, *Public Health Reports*, September 13, 1907, p. 1274.

"take action": telegram from President Theodore Roosevelt to Wyman, same as above.

CHAPTER THIRTEEN • BLUE'S BRIGADE (PAGE 128)

"Out of the houses . . .": "The Dream Rat," by Edward F. Cahill, *SF Call*, January 5, 1908.

"Plague was no longer . . .": Todd, p. 38.

"Where rats go . . .": "Introduction," by Walter Wyman, in *The Rat and Its Relation to the Public Health*, Public Health and Marine-Hospital Service of the United States, p. 14.

"When Dr. Blue . . .": "The Dream Rat," by Edward F. Cahill, *SF Call*, January 5, 1908.

"I intend . . .": Blue, quoted in "S. P. Men Hunt Rats," *SF Call*, February 19, 1908.

"I want you . . .": Dr. C. W. Rucker, quoted in "Public Health Up to People," *SF Call*, February 8, 1908.

"the success . . .": Wyman, quoted in Furman, p. 255.

"We needed . . .": Gillett, quoted in "Brilliant Banquet in Dr. Blue's Honor," *SF Call*, April 1, 1909.

"San Francisco has . . .": Blue, quoted in same as above.

"The disease . . .": Todd, p. 179.

CHAPTER FOURTEEN • INTO THE WILD (PAGE 140)

"Once planted . . .": "Rodents in Relation to the Transmission of Bubonic Plague," by Rupert Blue, in *The Rat and Its Relation to the Public Health*, Public Health and Marine-Hospital Service of the United States, p. 152.

"that the squirrels . . ." and "a most serious . . .": Blue, quoted in Furman, p. 254.

"The demonstration . . .": "Rodents in Relation to the Transmission of Bubonic Plague," by Rupert Blue, in Todd, p. 263.

"It would be surprising . . .": "Plague," SG 1914, p. 291.

CHAPTER FIFTEEN • DISEASE UNDEFEATED (PAGE 152)

"Recent outbreaks . . .": Dennis, p. 9.

"At that point . . .": Snow, quoted in "Colorado Girl on Road to Recovery after Suffering from Bubonic Plague," Rocky Mountain Hospital for Children, press release, January 1, 2014.

"It's one of those . . .": Drummond, quoted in "7-year-old Recovering from Bubonic Plague," 9news, Denver, Colorado, September 4, 2012.

"painful, red-hot . . ." and "They were coal . . .": Lucinda Marker, "We Survived the Bubonic Plague," Salon.com, July 15, 2012.

"If you know . . .": Paul Gaylord, "Experience: I Caught the Plague from My Cat," *Guardian*, January 31, 2014.

BIBLIOGRAPHY*

Abbott, Rachel C., and Tonie E. Rocke. *Plague: U.S. Geological Survey Circular 1372.* Reston, VA: U.S. Department of the Interior, U.S. Geological Survey, 2012.

Annual Report of the Department of Public Health of San Francisco, Cal. For the Fiscal Year Ending June 30, 1901. San Francisco: Hinton Printing Company, 1901.

Annual Report of the Supervising Surgeon-General of the Marine-Hospital Service of the United States. Fiscal Years 1900 and 1901. Washington, DC: Government Printing Office.

Annual Report of the Surgeon-General of the Public Health and Marine-Hospital Service of the United States. Fiscal Years 1902, 1903, 1904, 1905, 1906, 1907, 1909, 1910, 1911. Washington, DC: Government Printing Office.

Annual Report of the Surgeon General of the Public Health Service of the United States. Fiscal Year 1914. Washington, DC: Government Printing Office.

Benedict, Carol. *Bubonic Plague in Nineteenth-Century China.* Stanford, CA: Stanford University Press, 1996.

Benedictow, Ole J. *The Black Death, 1346–1353: The Complete History.* Rochester, NY: Boydell Press, 2004.

Biennial Report of the Board of Health of the City and County of San Francisco for the Fiscal Years 1898–1899 and 1899–1900. San Francisco: Hinton Printing Company, 1901.

Blue, Rupert. "Anti-Plague Measures in San Francisco, California, U.S.A." *Journal of Hygiene*, April 1909: 1–8.

Bollet, Alfred J. *Plagues and Poxes: The Impact of Human History on Epidemic Disease.* 2nd ed. New York: Demos, 2004.

Butler, Thomas. "Plague Gives Surprises in the First Decade of the 21st Century in the United States and Worldwide." *American Journal of Tropical Medicine and Hygiene*, October 2013: 788–93.

Chapin, Charles V. *The Sources and Modes of Infection.* New York: John Wiley and Sons, 1910.

*Websites active at time of publication

188

Chase, Marilyn. *The Barbary Plague: The Black Death in Victorian San Francisco.* New York: Random House, 2003.

Craddock, Susan. *City of Plagues: Disease, Poverty, and Deviance in San Francisco.* Minneapolis: University of Minnesota Press, 2000.

Crawford, Edward A., Jr. "Paul-Louis Simond and his Work on Plague." *Perspectives in Biology and Medicine,* Spring 1996: 446–58.

Dennis, David T., Kenneth L. Gage, Norman Gratz, Jack D. Poland, and Evgueni Tikhomirov. *Plague Manual: Epidemiology, Distribution, Surveillance and Control.* World Health Organization, 1999. who.int/csr/resources/publications/plague/WHO_CDS_CSR_EDC_99_2_EN/en/.

Duffy, John. *The Sanitarians: A History of American Public Health.* Urbana: University of Illinois Press, 1990.

Echenberg, Myron J. "Pestis Redux: The Initial Years of the Third Bubonic Plague Pandemic, 1894–1901." *Journal of World History,* Fall 2002: 429–49.

_____. *Plague Ports: The Global Urban Impact of Bubonic Plague, 1894–1901.* New York: New York University Press, 2007.

Furman, Bess. *A Profile of the United States Public Health Service, 1798–1948.* Washington, DC: U.S. Department of Health, Education, and Welfare; National Institutes of Health; and National Library of Medicine, 1973.

Gage, Kenneth L., and Michael Y. Kosoy. "Natural History of Plague: Perspectives from More than a Century of Research." *Annual Review of Entomology,* 2005: 505–28.

Gaylord, Paul. "Experience: I Caught the Plague from My Cat." *Guardian,* January 31, 2014. theguardian.com/lifeandstyle/2014/jan/31/i-caught-plague-from-my-cat?CMP=twt_gu.

Genthe, Arnold, and John Kuo Wei Tchen. *Genthe's Photographs of San Francisco's Old Chinatown.* New York: Dover Publications, 1984.

Gregg, Charles T. *Plague: An Ancient Disease in the Twentieth Century.* Albuquerque: University of New Mexico Press, 1985.

Gross, Ludwik. "How the Plague Bacillus and Its Transmission Through Fleas Were Discovered: Reminiscences from My Years at the Pasteur Institute in Paris." *Proceedings of the National Academy of Sciences of the United States of America,* August 1995: 7609–11.

Haas, Victor H. "When Bubonic Plague Came to Chinatown." *American Journal of Tropical Medicine and Hygiene,* March 1959: 141–47.

Hays, J. N. *Epidemics and Pandemics: Their Impacts on Human History.* Santa Barbara, CA: ABC-CLIO, 2005.

Kalisch, Philip A. "The Black Death in Chinatown: Plague and Politics in San Francisco 1900–1904." *Arizona and the West*, Summer 1972: 113–36.

Kazanjian, Powel. "Frederick Novy and the 1901 San Francisco Plague Commission Investigation." *Clinical Infectious Diseases*, November 15, 2012: 1373–78.

Kraut, Alan M. *Silent Travelers: Germs, Genes, and the "Immigrant Menace."* New York: Basic Books, 1994.

Kugeler, Kiersten J., J. Erin Staples, Alison F. Hinckley, Kenneth L. Gage, and Paul S. Mead. "Epidemiology of Human Plague in the United States, 1900–2012." *Emerging Infectious Diseases*, January 2015: 16–22.

Lamb, George, comp. *The Etiology and Epidemiology of Plague, A Summary of the Work of the Plague Commission*. Calcutta, India: Superintendent of Government Printing, 1908.

Link, Vernon B. *A History of Plague in the United States of America*. Washington, DC: Public Health Service, U.S. Department of Health, Education and Welfare, 1955.

Lipson, Loren George. "Plague in San Francisco in 1900." *Annals of Internal Medicine*, August 1972: 303–10.

Lutzker, Edythe, and Carol Jochnowitz. "The Curious History of Waldemar Haffkine." *Commentary*, June 1980: 61–64.

Markel, Howard. *When Germs Travel: Six Major Epidemics That Have Invaded America Since 1900 and the Fears They Have Unleashed*. New York: Random House, 2004.

Marker, Lucinda. "We Survived the Bubonic Plague." Salon.com, July 15, 2012. salon.com/2012/07/15/we_survived_the_bubonic_plague/.

Marriott, Edward. *Plague: A Story of Science, Rivalry, and the Scourge That Won't Go Away*. New York: Metropolitan Books, 2002.

McClain, Charles. "Of Medicine, Race, and American Law: The Bubonic Plague Outbreak of 1900." *Law and Social Inquiry*, Summer 1988: 447–513.

McNeill, William H. *Plagues and Peoples*. New York: Anchor Books, 1998.

Mead, Paul S. "*Yersinia* Species (Including Plague)." In *Mandell, Douglas, and Bennett's Principles and Practice of Infectious Diseases*, edited by John E. Bennett, Raphael Dolin, and Martin J. Blaser. 8th ed. Philadelphia: Saunders, 2015.

Morens, David M., Victoria A. Harden, Joseph Kinyoun Houts, Jr., and Anthony S. Fauci. *The Indispensable Forgotten Man: Joseph James Kinyoun and the Founding of the National Institutes of Health*. Washington, DC: National Institute of Allergy and Infectious Diseases, U.S. Department of Health and Human Services, 2012.

Mullan, Fitzhugh. *Plagues and Politics: The Story of the United States Public Health Service*. New York: Basic Books, 1989.

Nee, Victor G., and Brett de Bary Nee. *Longtime Californ': A Documentary Study of an American Chinatown*. New York: Pantheon Books, 1973.

Orent, Wendy. *Plague: The Mysterious Past and Terrifying Future of the World's Most Dangerous Disease*. New York: Free Press, 2004.

Perry, Robert D., and Jacqueline D. Fetherston. "*Yersinia pestis*—Etiologic Agent of Plague." *Clinical Microbiology Reviews*, January 1997: 35–66.

Pollitzer, R. *Plague*. World Health Organization Monograph Series, No. 22. Geneva: World Health Organization, 1954.

Public Health and Marine-Hospital Service of the United States. *The Rat and Its Relation to the Public Health*. Washington, DC: Government Printing Office, 1910.

Risse, Guenter B. *Plague, Fear, and Politics in San Francisco's Chinatown*. Baltimore, MD: Johns Hopkins University Press, 2012.

Shah, Nayan. *Contagious Divides: Epidemics and Race in San Francisco's Chinatown*. Berkeley: University of California Press, 2001.

Skubik, Mark M. "Public Health Politics and the San Francisco Plague Epidemic of 1900–1904." Master's Thesis, San Jose State University, 2002.

Todd, Frank Morton. *Eradicating Plague from San Francisco: Report of the Citizens' Health Committee and an Account of Its Work*. San Francisco: C. A. Murdock, 1909.

Transactions of the Association of American Physicians, Sixteenth Session, April 30 and May 1 and 2, 1901. Philadelphia: Association of American Physicians, 1901.

Wills, Christopher. *Yellow Fever, Black Goddess: The Coevolution of People and Plagues*. Reading, MA: Addison-Wesley, 1996.

Winslow, Charles-Edward Amory. *The Conquest of Epidemic Disease: A Chapter in the History of Ideas*. Princeton, NJ: Princeton University Press, 1944.

Wyman, Walter. *The Bubonic Plague*. Washington, DC: Government Printing Office, 1900.

Zinsser, Hans. *Rats, Lice, and History: Being a Study in Biography, Which, After Twelve Preliminary Chapters Indispensable for the Preparation of the Lay Reader, Deals with the Life History of Typhus Fever*. New York: Blue Ribbon Books, 1935.

Additional articles from these sources:
American Journal of Public Health
American Journal of Tropical Medicine and Hygiene
Bemidji [MN] Daily Pioneer
British Medical Journal
Bulletin of the History of Medicine
California History
California State Journal of Medicine
Evening Times [Grand Forks, ND]
Good Words
Guardian [U.S. edition]
Guthrie [OK] Daily Leader
Honolulu Star
Indianapolis [IN] Journal
Journal of Ancient Diseases & Preventive Remedies
Journal of Hygiene
Journal of Infectious Diseases
Journal of Medical Entomology
Journal of the American Medical Association
Lancet
Los Angeles Times
Military Surgeon
Morbidity and Mortality Weekly Report
9News [Denver, CO]
Occidental Medical Times
Pacific Medical Journal
Past and Present
Philadelphia Medical Journal
PLOS Medicine
Public Health Reports
Rocky Mountain Hospital for Children
Salon.com
San Francisco Call
San Francisco Chronicle
[Washington, D.C.] Times
Times of India
Washington Post
Western Journal of Medicine

INDEX

Page numbers in **boldface** refer to images and/or captions.

A

Angel Island, 67, 69, 70, **70**, 75, 80, 83, 85, 92, 106, 112, 179

B

Barker, Lewellys, 103, **103**, 105
Black Death, 8, 16–22, 170, 172, 174, 177
Blue, Rupert, **111**, 111–112, 116–117, 124–127, 130, **132**, 133–135, **137**, 137–138, **139**, 140–142, 144, 174
Bombay (Mumbai), India, **41**, 41–47, **43**, **47**, 49, 51–52, 64, 66
bubonic plague. *See* plague: bubonic (symptoms)

C

Canton (Guangzhou), China, 24–25, **25**, **26**, 27, 63, 73, 175
Centers for Disease Control and Prevention, 156, 176
Chinatown, San Francisco, California, **62**, 63–67, **65**, 77, **79**, **82**, **85**, 88–89, 100–102, 104–105, 116, **124**, **175**, 178
    cleanups and inspections, 66, 75, 80–81, 83–86, 108–109, 111, 114, 169
    living conditions, 63, **65**, 65–66
    quarantines, **2**, 64, 66, **66**, 71, **73**, 73–75, **75**, 78, **78**, 90–93, **91**, **92**, **94**, 95–96, 175, **175**
Chinese immigration, 65, **70**, 71, **71**, **72**, 73, 179
Chinese Six Companies, 73, 75, 88, 95, 104
Constantinople (Istanbul), Turkey, 13–14, 17
Contra Costa County, California, 115–116, 140–142

D

diphtheria, 31, 33, 34, 48, 68, 123, 172

F

fleas, **5**, **52**, **53**, **130**, 130–131, 133, **142**, 161, 169, 173
    plague vector, 52–55, 112, 116, 125, 127, 129, 132, 134, 136–137, 142, **142**, 144, **144**, **147**, 147–148, **148**, **150**, 150–151, **151**, 152–156, 158, 163–164, 167–171, 175.
    See also *Xenopsylla cheopis*
Flexner, Simon, 103, **103**

G

Gage, Henry T., 93, 97–98, 102, **102**, 105–106, 108–110, 117

H

Haffkine, Waldemar, 44–47, **45**, 49, 175
Hare, Charles, 117
Hong Kong, **27**, 27–37, **28**, **29**, **30**, **37**, 39–40, **40**, 42, 56, 66, 69–70, 103, 175
Honolulu, Hawaii, **56**, 56–60, **57**, **58**, **59**, 64, 66, 69, 73, 175
Ho Yow, 73, 75, 78, 88, 92

J

Jew Ho lawsuit, 95
Justinian I, 15, **15**, 174

K

Karachi (Pakistan), **42**, 44, **44**
Kellogg, Wilfred, 63–64, 67, 79
Kinyoun, Joseph, 67–69, **68**, 71, 74–78, **78**, 80, 83–89, **87**, 91–93, **96**, 96–106, **98**, **102**, **104**, **106**, **107**, 108, 110, 112, 174–175, 178
Kitasato, Shibasaburo, **32**, 32–38, **35**, 55, 68
Koch, Robert, 31, 32, 34, **47**, 68, 103

L

Los Angeles, California, 110, 144–146, 156, 175
Lowson, James, 33–36, 38

M

Manchuria, China, **164**, 164–165, **165**
McKinley, William, 87, 98, 102, 105, **105**
Morrow, William, 88–90, 95–99, **98**

N

newspapers, 41, **71**, **72**, 83–85, 101, 104–106, 108, 119, **120**, **121**, 178
    San Francisco press, 63–64, **66**, **74**, 74–75, **75**, **78**, **81**, 83–84, 86–87, **87**, 92–93, 95, **96**, 97–98, **98**, **102**, **104**, 104–105, **106**, **107**, **110**, **120**, **132**, 134
Niles, Mary, 24–25, 27, 39
Novy, Frederick, **103**, 103–104, 117

O

O'Brien, A. P., 64, 66
Ogata, Masanori, 55, 66, 125, 175

P

Pardee, George, 110, **110**
Pasteur, Louis, 31, **31**, 33–34, 68, 103
Pasteur Institute, 34, 36–38, 45, **48**, 48–49, 51, 77
plague
    in animals, 141–142, 145–148, **147**, **148**, **149**, 156, **158**, 167, 175
        cats, 155, **159**, 159–160, 167
        gerbils, 148
        ground squirrels, **140**, 140–146, **142**, **143**, 148, 152–153, 175
        marmots, 148, 164
        prairie dogs, 148, **149**, 155, **165**, 166, **166**, **167**. *See also* rats; fleas
    bioweapon, 16, 163–164, 172
    bubonic (symptoms), 8–9, **10–11**, 13, **17**, 17–18, 24–25, 27, 56, 63–64, 69, **69**, 84, 100, 115, 152–154, 158, 160, **171**, 172, 176–177
    cause of
        early beliefs, 14, 18, 20–21, 27–28
        scientific explanation, 153–155, 176–177.
            See also *Yersinia pestis*

current research, **165**, 165–166, 177
diagnosis, 56, 64, 69, 71, 76–77, 80, 84, 99, 100, 104–105, 115, 117, 158, 168, 176–177
fatality rates, 9, 14–15, 22, 27, 30–31, 44, 59–60, 101, 109, 116, 136, 143, 144, 146, 154, 156, 161–162, 165, 169–171
outbreaks, 1950s to present, 152–163, **157**, **161**, **162**, **171**
pandemics
    First (Justinian), 13–15, **15**, 169, 170–171, **171**, 174
    Second, **13**, **16**, 16–22, **17**, **19**, **20**, **21**, **23**, 169, 170–171, **171**, 174. *See also* Black Death
    Third, 25, 27, 31, 60, 69, 117–118, **118**, **144**, 161, 169, 174
        China, 161, **164**, 164–165, **165**, 169. *See also* Canton (Guangzhou), China; Hong Kong
        India, 44, 48, 161, 169. *See also* Bombay (Mumbai), India; Karachi (Pakistan)
        United States, 69–70, 140–146, **143**, **145**, 156. *See also* Honolulu, Hawaii; Los Angeles, California; San Francisco, California
pneumonic (symptoms), 9, 17, 100, 117, 155–156, 159–160, 164–165, 168, 173, 176–177
prevention, 18, **20**, 20–21, **21**, 55, **155**, 167, 168
    flea control, 125, 127, **130**, 132, 144, 161, 163, 169, 171, 175
    Haffkine vaccine, 46–49, 57, 60, 78, 84–86, 88–89, 97, 127, 171, 175
    rodent control, 92, 112, 114, **114**, 127, **130**, 130–137, **131**, **132**, **135**, **136**, 142, **143**, 144, **145**, 146, 161, 166, **169**, 171
    sanitary campaigns, 28, **29**, **42**, 42–43, **44**, **57**, 57–59, **58**, **59**, 66, 75, **75**, 80–81, 83–86, 91, 109, 111–112
    ship inspections, **69**, 69–71, **70**, 77, 83, 88, 132, 144
    travel restrictions, 21, 43, 83, 87–89, **89**, **96**, 96–99, 165
    Yersin serum, 49, 60, 78, 109, 127, 171, 175
septicemic (symptoms), 9, **11**, 13, 17, 100, 154–155, 158, 160, 173, 176–177
symptoms. *See* plague: bubonic; plague: pneumonic; plague: septicemic

transmission, 39, 126, 145–146, 148, 154–156, **155**, 159–160, 164–165, 168.
    See also fleas: plague vector
        early beliefs, 18, 20, 28, 39–40, 52, 66
    treatment
        antibiotics, 153–156, 158, 160–161, 164, 166, 168, 171, 172, 175, 176–177
        medieval, 18
        Yersin serum, 49, **50**, 51, **51**, 57, 60, 78, 101, 117, 126, 171, 175
Procopius, 13–14

Q

quarantine, 21, 28, 40, 42, 51, 55, 56–57, **57**, 59, 61, 69–70, **70**, 105, 173, 177. *See also* Chinatown, San Francisco, California: quarantines

R

rats, **35**, **55**, **108**, **112**, **118**, 141, 169, **171**, **175**
    autopsies of, **113**, **133**, 133–134, 137, **137**
    control of. *See* plague: prevention: rodent control
    fleas, relationship with. *See* fleas: plague vector
    omen of plague, 24–25, 41, 123, 134
    plague transmission, role in, 39–40, 51–55, 58–59, 91, 112, 116–118, 125, 138, 142, 144, **144**, 146, 148, 156, 163, **171**
Roosevelt, Theodore, 123–124
Roux, Émile, 33–34, **34**, 68

S

San Francisco, California, **62**, **63**, 68–71, 73–75, 178–179
    Board of Health and health department, 66–67, 73–75, **75**, 77–81, 83–85, **85**, 87–88, 90–91, 93, 95–96, 99, 100, 102, 105, 108, 112, 117, 175.
        See also Kellogg, Wilfred; O'Brien, A.P.; Williamson, John
    Citizens' Health Committee, 135, **135**, 138, **139**
    court decisions, 88–90, 95–99
    earthquake, 1906, **119**, 119–125, **120**, **121**, **122**, **124**, **125**, **126**, **128**, 174, **174**, 178–179
    plague commission of 1901, **103**, 103–106, **104**, 117, 174

plague laboratory, 108, 112, **113**, **115**, 116–117, **133**, 133–134, 136–137, **137**, 141–142
plague outbreaks
    1900–1904, 63–117, 174–175
    1907–1909, 123–138, 174–175.
    See also Angel Island; Chinatown, San Francisco, California
Simond, Paul-Louis, **50**, **51**, 51–55, 66, 125, 175
Soto, Matilda, 115–117, 140

T

typhoid fever, 28, 31, 86, 99, 105, 123, 173

U

U.S. Marine-Hospital Service (Public Health Service), 69, 85, 88, 93, 103–104, 106, 108, 110, **112**, 123, **137**, 137–138, 169
    history of, 61, 68, **68**.
    See also Angel Island; Blue, Rupert; Kinyoun, Joseph; San Francisco, California: plague laboratory; Wyman, Walter

W

White, Joseph, 108
Williamson, John, 80, 106
Wong Chut King, 63–67, 70–71, 73, 75, 77–78, 80, 156, 175
Wong Wai lawsuit, 88, 97, **98**, 99
Wyman, Walter, 39, 51, 60, **60**, 68, 76–78, 80, 84–85, 87, 97–99, 101–103, 105–106, 108–109, 111, 117, 124, 138

X

Xenopsylla cheopis (Oriental rat flea), **53**, 54, 150–151, **151**, 169

Y

Yersin, Alexandre, 32–39, **33**, **36**, **37**, 48–49, 51, 175
Yersinia pestis (plague bacteria), **36**, 38, **38**, 69, **115**, 142, 144–148, 150–151, **151**, **153**, 153–155, 158–161, 163, 165–171, **168**, **169**
    description, 37, **168**
    discovery, 36–39, 171, 175

PICTURE CREDITS

Annual Report of the Supervising Surgeon-General of the Marine-Hospital Services of the United States, Fiscal Year 1896: 70.

Courtesy of **The Bancroft Library, University of California, Berkeley**, from *The Wave*, June 16, 1900, xffF850.W186 v. 21:no.21: 07 [7]: 91; xffF850.W186 v. 21:no.21: 07 [4]: 92; xffF850.W186 v. 21:no.21: [cover]: 94.

Lewellys F. Barker. *Time and the Physician*. New York: G. P. Putnam's Sons, 1942: 103.

Centers for Disease Control and Prevention: 157 (top and bottom), 161, 171 (bottom); Public Health Image Library: 5, 10 (top, bottom left and right), 11 (top left and right, bottom), 37, 38, 52 (left and right), 53, 55, 142 (top and bottom), 147, 149 (top left and right), 151 (top), 153, 168, 169 (bottom), 171 (top).

Flickr (Creative Commons Attribution-ShareAlike 2.0): Rat surmulot/Brown Rat by Jean-Jacques Boujot: front flap, 175 (bottom); "Eyam Tomb" by Duncan: 12; "Norway Rat on a Barrel" by Bayer CropScience UK: 108.

Frank Leslie's Illustrated Newspaper, April 1, 1882: 71; November 20, 1880: 72.

Gainesville [FL] Daily Sun, April 19, 1906: 120 (bottom right).

Guthrie [OK] Daily Leader, April 18, 1906: 121 (top right).

Harper's Weekly, June 2, 1900: 2, 73; June 3, 1899: 41.

Hawaii State Archives: 56, 57 (top and bottom), 58, 59 (top and bottom).

iStock.com/Antagain: front jacket (rats), 3.

Library of Congress, Prints and Photographs Division, LC-USZ62-54324: 25; LC-USZ62-54329: 26; LC-USZ62-61011: 28; LC-USZ62-118820: 30; LC-USZ62-118532: 40; LC-USZ62-70343: 62; LC-USZ62-70338: 65 (top); LC-USZ62-33526: 89; LC-DIG-ppmsca-09832: 119; LC-USZ62-96789: 120 (top); LC-DIG-ppmsca-09835: 125; LC-USZ62-101015: 128; LC-USZ62-47590: 174; Arnold Genthe Collection: LC-G403-0187: 65 (bottom); LC-G4033-0199: 79; LC-G403-0053: 82; LC-USZ62-136179: 85; LC-G403-T-0175-A: 175 (top); Detroit Publishing Company Photograph Collection: LC-D4-19246: 124; Frances Benjamin Johnston Collection: LC-USZ62-83133: 105; Frank and Frances Carpenter Collection, LC-USZ62-118505: 27; George Grantham Bain Collection, LC-B2-3787-3: 35; LC-B2-2178-11: 164.

National Archives and Records Administration: 121 (bottom), 122, 126.

National Institutes of Health: 151 (bottom).

National Library of Medicine, History of Medicine Collection: 16, 60, 68, 111, 112, 113, 114, 115, 130 (top), 130–131 (bottom), 131 (top), 133, 137 (top and bottom), 139, 143, 145.

National Museum of Health and Medicine: 155; Otis Historical Archives: 150.

Paducah [KY] Sun, April 20, 1906: 121 (top left).

Pixabay: 167.

San Francisco Call, March 9, 1900: 66, 74 (right); March 8, 1900: 74 (left); March 10, 1900: 75 (top); March 11, 1900: 75 (bottom); March 13, 1900: 78, 81; March 20, 1900: 87; June 17, 1900: 96; June 19, 1900: 98; January 9, 1901: 102 (top and bottom); February 1, 1901: 104; April 16, 1901: 107; November 4, 1902: 110 (top); November 5, 1902: 110 (bottom); March 1, 1908: 132 (top and bottom).

San Francisco Call-Chronicle-Examiner, April 19, 1906: 120 (bottom left).

Shutterstock.com/Mega Pixel: front jacket (newspaper stack), 3.

N. C. Stenseth, B. B. Atshabar, M. Begon, S. R. Belmain, E. Bertherat, et al. "Plague: Past, Present, and Future." *PLOS Medicine*, January 2008: 148, 162.

Papers of **Richard P. Strong** (GA82.3, slide A-41), Harvard Medical Library in the Francis A. Countway Library of Medicine: 165 (top).

Frank Morton Todd. *Eradicating Plague from San Francisco: Report of the Citizens' Health Committee and an Account of Its Work*. San Francisco: C. A. Murdock, 1909: 135, 136, 169 (top).

United States Fish and Wildlife Service: 140, 149 (bottom), 159.

United States Geological Survey: 165 (bottom); photo by Marisa Lubeck: 166.

Wellcome Library, London: 19, 20 (top and bottom), 21, 23, 29, 32, 33, 34, 36, 42, 43, 44, 45 (top and bottom), 47, 48, 50, 69; drawing by A. L. Tarter: 118, 144.

Wikimedia Commons (Creative Commons Attribution-ShareAlike 2.0): 15, 17, 31.

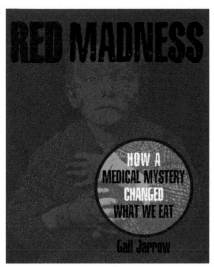

Ages 10 and up
Grades 5 and up
Hardcover • $16.95 U.S./$21.50 CAN
978-1-59078-732-8
e-book • $9.99 • 978-1-62979-215-6
Calkins Creek

★ "This title is descriptive and well researched, with a striking bold-red color scheme. Though the images are graphic and potentially disturbing, they are not sensationalized, and enhance the narrative. This is an excellent addition to nonfiction collections in school and public libraries."
—School Library Journal, starred review

★ "This is a highly detailed look at the difficulties of disease control before modern medicine. . . . The attractive, red-highlighted design, lively narrative and compelling subject matter will resonate with readers."
—Kirkus Reviews, starred review

"A visually dramatic medical mystery, this is cross-curricular and of high interest." **—Booklist**

A *School Library Journal* Best Book of the Year

Jefferson Cup Award for Older Readers

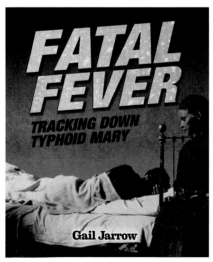

Ages 10 and up
Grades 5 and up
Hardcover • $16.95 U.S./$21.50 CAN
978-1-62091-597-4
e-book • $9.99 • 978-1-62979-060-2
Calkins Creek

★ "Captivating. . . . Replete with archival photos, this thorough account brings readers to the present day and modern medicine's fight against what is still a scourge in many countries."
—Publishers Weekly, starred review

★ "A nonfiction page-turner relying upon extensive research and copious source notes, this is a fantastic addition to any library."
—School Library Journal, starred review

★ "Readers who are curious about Typhoid Mary . . . will find this an absorbing account of what actually happened." **—Booklist, starred review**

★ "A top-notch addition to the popular topic of deadly diseases."
—Kirkus Reviews, starred review

GAIL JARROW merges biology and history in her third medical mystery about deadly diseases in early twentieth-century America. Her books have received numerous awards and distinctions, including a YALSA Award Nomination for Excellence in Nonfiction, an Orbis Pictus recommendation, the Jefferson Cup Award, and a National Science Teachers Association recommended title. Gail has a degree in zoology and has taught science to students of all ages. She lives in Ithaca, New York. Visit her at gailjarrow.com.